UPON A PENNY LOAF

UPONA PENNY LOAF

The wisdom of JOHN BUNYAN, author of Pilgrim's Progress

compiled by ROGER C. PALMS

editor of *Decision Magazine*

Bethany Fellowship INC.
MINNEAPOLIS, MINNESOTA 55438

Published by Bethany Fellowship, Inc.
6820 Auto Club Road, Minneapolis, Minnesota 55438

Printed in the United States of America

Library of Congress Cataloging in Publication Data

Bunyan, John, 1623-1688.
   Upon a penny loaf.

   Includes index.
   1. Christian literature, English—Collected works.
I. Palms, Roger C. II. Title.
BR75. B7 1978   230   78-12239
ISBN 0-87123-573-0

Preface

In his own words John Bunyan explains what he intends to show us through his writings:

"In this discourse of mine you may see much of the grace of God toward me. I thank God I can count it much.

"Moses wrote of the journeyings of the children of Israel from Egypt to the land of Canaan, and commanded also that they remember all the ways which the Lord leads. This I have endeavored to do; and not only so but also to publish it so that if God wills, others may be put in remembrance of what he has done for their souls—by reading of his work upon me."

Bunyan speaks of value—the value of a person, the value of God's Word and the value of God's grace. In his poem, "Upon a Penny Loaf," he says:

Your price one penny is in time of plenty;
In famine, doubled, 'tis from one to twenty.
Yea, no man knows what price on you to set
When there is but one penny loaf to get.

That great price is what his writings—and this book you hold in your hand—are all about.

Introduction

John Bunyan was a tinker, a mender of pots, in Bedford, England. What God did with him is a story that is perhaps unmatched by any other in history. Today, 300 years after he lived, his wisdom speaks to the whole world. Next to the Bible, his books have outsold every other published work.

Bunyan's birth was not exceptional; few took notice of it. In fact, no one even knows the proper spelling of his name. Records in the Elstow Parish Church list his birth as: "John, the sonne of Thos. Bonnion, Jurr. 30th November, 1628."

He was an intense red-headed young man who, as he tells it, lived a pagan life: "It was my delight to be taken captive by the devil at his will, being filled with all unrighteousness. Yea, so settled and rooted was I in these things that they became second nature to me."

But for John Bunyan a new life was coming. At age 19 he met a young woman and married her. This woman (no one knows her name) was a quiet instrument in his eventual conversion to Christ. Bunyan says: "My mercy was to light upon a wife whose father was counted godly. This woman and I, though we came together as poor as poor might be (not having so much household stuff as a dish or a spoon between us both), yet she had for her part *The Plain Man's Pathway to Heaven* and *The Practice of Piety* which her father had left her when he died. In these two books which I sometimes read with her, I found some things that were somewhat pleasing to me. But all this while I met with no conviction. These books, though they did not reach my heart to awaken it, yet they did beget within me some desire to reform my vicious life."

Bunyan began to wrestle with God—and God won. "I felt my own heart begin to shake, for I saw that in all my thoughts about religion and salvation the new birth had never entered my mind. Neither knew I the comfort of the word and promise, nor the deceitfulness and treachery of my own wicked heart.

"Could salvation have been gotten for gold, what I would have given for it! If I had a whole world, it would have all gone ten thousand times over for this so that my soul might have been in a converted state.

"I began to give place to the Word, and with that my heart was filled full of comfort and hope. Now I could believe that my sins would be forgiven me. Yea, I was now so taken with the love and mercy of God that I remember that I could not tell how to contain till I got home. I thought I could have spoken of his love and told of his mercy to me even to the crows that sat on the plowed lands before me. I said in my soul, I wish I had a pen and ink here; I would write this down before I go any farther. Surely I will not forget this forty years hence."

When the battle was ended and he knew that he had taken the gift of life offered by Jesus Christ, the tinker from Bedford began to preach.

"Sometimes, when some went into the country to teach, they asked me to go with them. Though as yet

I did not make use of my gift in an open way, still, as I came among the people in those places, I did sometimes speak a word of admonition to them. They received it, rejoicing at the mercy of God toward me, professing their souls were edified thereby.

"Therefore, after some solemn prayer to the Lord, I was more particularly called forth to a public preaching of the Word, not only to them that believed but also to offer the gospel to those who had not yet received the faith. I did not preach long before some began to be touched and to be greatly afflicted in their minds at the apprehension of the greatness of their sin and of their need of Jesus Christ.

"In my preaching I was really in pain to bring forth children to God. I was not satisfied unless some fruit did appear in my work. If I were fruitless, it mattered not who commended me, but if I were fruitful, I cared not who condemned. It pleased me not at all to see people drink in my opinions if they seemed ignorant of Jesus Christ. The worth of their own salvation, the sound conviction for sin, a heart set on fire to be saved by Christ, the strong breathings after a truly sanctified soul—that was what delighted me."

But Bunyan didn't preach very long before he was arrested and imprisoned. Preaching the gospel outside of the established church was against the law. That law didn't stop him, however, nor did he even try to escape the authorities. He said to his friends, "Come, be of good cheer; let us not be daunted. Our cause is good; we need not be ashamed of it. To preach God's Word is so good a work that we shall be well rewarded if we suffer for it. If I should now run and escape, what would my weak and newly converted brethren think of it?"

He was to stay in Bedford jail, with the exception of a brief release, for the next twelve years. Then in 1672, he was freed under the Declaration of Indulgence.

It was during those twelve prison years that he studied the Scriptures and wrote many of his now famous works. Of his time in prison, Bunyan said: "I begged God that if I might do more good being at liberty than in prison, that then I might be set at liberty, but if not, his will be done. For I was not altogether without hope that my imprisonment might be an awakening to the saints in the country; therefore I could not tell which to choose. I did commit the thing to God. And I did meet my God sweetly in prison, comforting me and satisfying me that it was his will and mind that I should be there."

Following his release, Bunyan remained in Bedford village as a pastor until he died, August 31, 1688.

Although John Bunyan is best known for two particular books, *The Pilgrim's Progress* and *Grace Abounding*, he produced over sixty other works. In the following pages, the great thoughts of Bunyan have been selected and edited from his entire published collection.

To read Bunyan is to join millions of people who have had their lives enriched by his wisdom—the wisdom of a simple tinker touched by the grace of God.

Table of Contents

Chapter One

A PROSPEROUS JOURNEY

"Christ, and Christ only, can make us capable of enjoying God with life and joy for all eternity."

If you do not know the way, inquire at the Word of God. If you want company, cry for God's Spirit. If you want encouragement, entertain the promises. But be sure that you begin. Get into the way, run apace, and hold out to the end, and the Lord give you a prosperous journey.   —*The Heavenly Footman*

I believe that the Prince under whose banner I now stand is able to absolve me, and to pardon what I did in my compliance with you, O destroying Apollyon. To speak the truth, I like his service, his wages, his servants, his government, his company and country, better than yours. Therefore, stop trying to persuade me further; I am his servant and I will follow him.

—*The Pilgrim's Progress*

The whole Bible was given for this very end, that you should both believe this doctrine and live in the comfort and sweetness of it.   —*Christian Behavior*

The man who is full of good works is fit to live and fit to die. But he who is barren is neither fit to live nor fit to die. To die, he himself is convinced he is not fit, and to live, God himself says he is not fit: "Cut it down; why cumbereth it the ground?" (Luke 13:7).   —*Christian Behavior*

Men are subject to two extremes, either to confess sins notionally and by halves, or else, together with the confession of them, to labor to do some holy work to ease their burdened consciences and beget faith in the mercy of God. Now both of these are dangerous and very ungodly: dangerous, because the wound is healed falsely; and ungodly, because the command is transgressed. Only acknowledge your sin and there stand till your guilt is taken away.
                —*Justification by an Imputed Righteousness*

Barren soul, how many showers of grace, how many dews from heaven, how many times have the silver streams of the city of God run gliding by your roots, to cause you to bring forth fruit? These showers and streams and the drops that hang upon your boughs will all be accounted for. Will they not testify against you? Hear and tremble, O you barren professor. The God of heaven expects fruits that become your profession of the gospel.   —*The Barren Fig Tree*

The cross stands, and has stood from the beginning, as a way-mark to the kingdom of heaven. If one asks you the way to such and such a place, you do not only say, "This is the way," but you also say, "You must go by such a gate, by such a stile, such a bush, tree, bridge, or such like." And so it is here. Are you inquiring the way to heaven? I tell you, Christ is the way; into him you must get, into his righteousness, to be justified. And if you are in him, you will presently see the cross. You must go close by it, you must touch it, you must take it up, or else you will quickly go out of the way that leads to heaven and turn up some of those crooked lanes which lead down to the chambers of death.　　　　　*—The Heavenly Footman*

Christ, and Christ only, can make us capable of enjoying God with life and joy for all eternity. Hence he calls himself the way to the Father, and the true and living way. We cannot come to the Father except by him. Satan knows this; therefore, he hates him. Deluded persons are ignorant of this, and that's why they are so led up and down by Satan by the nose as they are.　　　　　*—The Jerusalem Sinner Saved*

Where can you find that God was ever false to his promise, or that he ever deceived the soul that ventured itself upon him? He often calls upon sinners to trust him, though they walk in darkness and have no light.
　　　　　—The Jerusalem Sinner Saved

Be willing to hear and learn and obey those whom God, by his providence, has set over you. This is a great means to perserve the unity and peace of churches. When men usurp authority, and think themselves wiser than their teachers, they run into contentions and parties. This is the first step to schism and is usually attended, if not timely prevented, with a sinful separation.

If you would keep the unity of the Spirit in the bond of peace, be aware that the God whom you serve is a God of Peace, and your Savior is a Prince of Peace. "His ways are ways of pleasantness, and all his paths are peace" (Prov. 3:17). Christ was sent into the world to give light to them that sit in darkness and in the shadow of death, and to guide our feet in the way of peace.

Consider the oneness of spirit that is among the enemies of religion. Though they differ about other things, yet to persecute religion and eradicate it from the earth they will agree. The devils in the air, and the devils in the earth, and all the devils in hell and in the world, are as one in this. Shall the devil's kingdom be united, and Christ's be divided? Shall the devils make one shoulder to drive on the design of damning men, and shall not Christians unite to carry on the great design of saving them?

—The Jerusalem Sinner Saved

Many Christians live in this world as if religion was
but a by-business and this world the one thing neces-
sary, when indeed all the things of this world are but
things by the by, and religion only the one thing needful.   —*Christian Behavior*

The hill, though high, I covet to ascend;
The difficulty will not me offend
For I perceive the way to life lies here.
Come, pluck up, heart; let's neither faint nor fear.
Better, though difficult, the right way to go
Than wrong, though easy, where the end is woe.
                          —*The Pilgrim's Progress*

Then said the man, "Neighbors, wherefore are ye
come?"

They said, "To persuade you to go back with us."

But he said, "That can by no means be; you dwell
in the City of Destruction, the place also where I was
born. I see it to be so. And dying there, sooner or
later you will sink lower than the grave into a place
that burns with fire and brimstone. Be content, good
neighbors, and go along with me."

"What," said Obstinate, "and leave our friends and
comforts behind us?"

"Yes," said Christian (for that was his name), " because all which you shall forsake is not worthy to be
compared with a little of that which I am seeking to
enjoy. And if you will go along with me, and hold it,.
you shall fare as myself, for there where I go is enough
and to spare.   —*The Pilgrim's Progress*

I see myself now at the end of my journey; my toilsome days are ended. I am going to see that head that was crowned with thorns, and the face that was spit upon for me. I have formerly lived by hearsay and faith, but now I go where I shall live by sight and shall be with him in whose company I delight myself. —*The Pilgrim's Progress, Part II*

Christian, make your profession shine by a conversation according to the gospel, or else you will damnify religion, bring scandal to your brethren, and give offence to the enemies. It would be better that a millstone was hanged around your neck and that, so adorned, you were cast into the sea, than so to do.

Christian, a profession according to the gospel is, in these days, a rare thing. Seek after it, put it on, and keep it without spot, and you shall be a rare Christian.

Now God Almighty give his people grace not to hate or malign sinners nor yet to choose any of their ways, but to keep themselves pure from the blood of all men by speaking and doing according to that name, and those rules, that they profess to know and love, for Jesus Christ's sake. —*The Author to the Reader*

Will he who does not believe the testimony of Christ concerning the baseness of sin and the insufficiency of the righteousness of the world come to Christ for life? No!

He who does not believe the testimony of the Word comes not. He who believes that there is life anywhere else comes not. He who questions whether the Father has given Christ power to forgive comes not. He who thinks that there is more in sin, in the law, in death, and in the devil to destroy, than there is in Christ to save, comes not. He also who questions Christ's faithful management of his priesthood for the salvation of sinners comes not.   —*Come, and Welcome, to Jesus Christ*

Barren fig tree, do you hear? God expects fruit. God calls for fruit. God will shortly come seeking fruit on this barren fig tree. Barren fig tree, either bear fruit or go out of the vineyard.   —*The Barren Fig Tree*

Chapter Two
SOME NICE, FOOLISH CURIOSITIES

"What folly can be greater than to labor for the meat that perishes and neglect the food of eternal life?"

Do not be looking too high in your journey heavenward. Men who run a race do not stare and gaze this way and that, neither do they cast up their eyes too high lest through their too much gazing after other things they stumble and fall. The very same case is this: If you gaze and stare after every opinion and way that comes into the world, you may stumble and fall. If you pry too much into God's secret decrees, or let your heart too much entertain questions about some nice, foolish curiosities, you may stumble and fall.

—The Heavenly Footman

Love not the world, for it is a moth in a Christian's life.

—Bunyan's Dying Sayings (of the Love of the World)

The reason why the poor world does not earnestly desire mercy is partly because people do not seriously consider the torment into which they must certainly fall if they die out of Christ. For, let me tell you, if poor souls indeed considered the wrath which does by right fall because of their sins against God, they would make more haste to God for mercy than they do. *—The Groans of a Damned Soul*

Some people are so deluded by the devil as to think that God is so merciful that he will regard anything as prayer. Through ignorance they think that if they mutter some form of prayer, though they know not what they say nor what they request, God is satisfied. I beseech you to seek in good earnest for the Spirit of Christ to help you strive and pray. Lay hold on Christ that your souls may be saved.
—The Groans of a Damned Soul

Mercy seems to be out of its proper channel when it deals with self-righteous men, but runs with a full stream when it extends itself to the biggest sinners. God's mercy is not regulated by man's goodness, nor obtained by man's worthiness.
—The Jerusalem Sinner Saved

All works are not good that seem to be so. It is one thing for a man's ways to be right in his own eyes, and another for them to be right in God's. Often that which is of high estimation with men is an abomination in the sight of God. *—Christian Behavior*

He who heartily confesses his sin is like him who, hearing a thief or traitor in his house, brings him out to take the punishment. But he that forbears to confess is like him who hides a thief or traitor against the laws and peace of our Lord the King.

—*Instruction for the Ignorant*

Peter little thought that he had cursing, swearing, lying, and an inclination in his heart to deny his Master before the temptation came. But when that came upon him, he found it there to his sorrow.

Some that are coming to Jesus Christ are too much affected with their own graces and too little taken with Christ's person. Therefore God, to take them off from doting on their own jewels so that they might look more to the person, undertaking, and merits of his Son, plunges them into the ditch by temptations.

—*Come, and Welcome, to Jesus Christ*

Pride, where it comes and is entertained, is a certain forerunner of some judgment that is not far behind. When pride goes before, shame and destruction will follow after.   —*The Life and Death of Mr. Badman*

'Tis strange to see how over-nice are some
About their clothes, their bodies, and their homes;
While what's of worth they slightly pass it by,
Not doing it at all, or slovenly.

Their houses must well furnish'd be in print,
While their immortal soul has no good in't.
Its outside also they must beautify,
While there is in't scarce common honesty.

Their bodies they must have trick'd up and trim;
Their inside full of filth up to the brim.
Upon their clothes there must not be a spot,
Whereas their lives are but a common blot.

How nice, how coy, are some about their diet
That can their crying souls with hog's-meat quiet.
All must be drest to a hair or else 'tis naught,
While of the living bread they have no thought.
—Upon Over-much Niceness

The Frog by nature is both damp and cold;
Her mouth is large, her belly much will hold.
She sits somewhat ascending, loves to be
Croaking in gardens, tho' unpleasantly.

Comparison

The hypocrite is like unto this Frog,
As like as is the puppy to the dog.
He is of nature cold; his mouth is wide
To prate, and at true godliness to deride.
And tho' the world is that which has his love,
He mounts his bed as if he lived above.
And though he seeks in churches for to croak,
He neither loveth Jesus nor his yoke.
—Upon the Frog

The hen so soon as she an egg doth lay
Spreads the fame of her doing what she may.
About the yard a cackling she doth go
To tell what 'twas she at her nest did do.

Just so it is with some professing men;
If they do aught that's good they, like our hen,
Cannot but cackle on't where-e'er they go,
And what their right hand doth, their left must know.
                    —*On the Cackling of a Hen*

Nothing more hinders a soul from coming to Christ
than a vain love of the world. And until a soul is
free from it, it can never have a true love for God.
    —*Bunyan's Dying Sayings (of the Love of the World)*

To slight grace, to despise mercy, and to stop the
ear when God speaks such great things to our profit
is a great provocation.

He offers, he calls, he woos, he invites, he prays,
he beseeches us, in this day of his grace, to be reconciled to him, and has provided for us the means of
reconciliation to himself. Now when this is despised,
it must be provoking, and "it is a fearful thing to fall
into the hands of the living God" (Heb. 10:31).
                    —*The Jerusalem Sinner Saved*

Be careful of driving so hard after this world that you hinder yourself and your family from those duties towards God to which you are by grace obliged: private prayer, reading the Scriptures, and Christian conference. It is a base thing for men so to spend themselves and their families after this world that they disengage their hearts from God's worship.

—Christian Behavior

What folly can be greater than to labor for the meat that perishes and neglect the food of eternal life?

—Bunyan's Dying Sayings (of the Love of the World)

Take heed that a sin in your life does not go unrepented, for that will make a flaw in your living, a wound in your conscience, and a breach in your peace. It may at last drive all the grace in you into so dark a corner of your heart that you shall not be able, by all the torches that are burning in the gospel, to find it.

—The Strait Gate

Behold how eager our little boy
Is for this butterfly, as if all joy,
All profits, honors, and lasting pleasures,
Were wrapt up in her—or the richest treasures
Found in her—
When her all is lighter than a feather.

He halloos, runs, and cries out, "Here, boys, here."
Nor doth he brambles or the nettles fear.
He stumbles at the molehills; up he gets,
And runs again, as one bereft of wits,
While all his labor and this large outcry
Is only for a silly butterfly.

This little boy is much like those
Whose hearts are wholly at the world's dispose.
The butterfly does represent to me
The world's best things, at best but fading be.
All are but painted nothings and false joys,
Like this poor butterfly to these our boys.
His running through the nettles, thorns and briars
To gratify his boyish fond desires;
His tumbling over molehills to attain
His end, namely his butterfly to gain,
Plainly shows what hazards some men run
To get what will be lost as soon as won.
Men seem, in choice, than children far more wise
Because they run not after butterflies,
When yet, alas, for what are empty toys
They follow them, and act as beardless boys.
                    —*Of the Boy and His Butterfly*

In my lifetime (said the rich man in hell) I did not care to hear that word that cut me most and showed my estate aright. I was vexed to hear my sins mentioned and laid to my charge. I loved him best who deceived me most, he who said, "Peace, peace," when there was no such thing. But, oh, that I had been told of it! It is better to be dealt with plainly than that we should be deceived; men had better see their lost condition in the world than to be damned.

—The Groans of a Damned Soul

Chapter Three

IF THE HEART RUNS WITH THE TONGUE

"Prayer is one of the first things that proves a man to be a Christian."

he Lord awaken you and learn you, poor souls, in all humility, to take heed that you are not rash or unadvised with your hearts, and much more with your mouths, when you appear before God. It must be a prayer with the Spirit if it is to be accepted, because there is nothing but the Spirit that can lift up the soul or heart to God in prayer. If the heart runs with the tongue, it must be prepared by the Spirit of God.

—Discourse on Prayer

When you pray, rather let your heart be without words than your words be without a heart.

—Bunyan's Dying Sayings (of Prayer)

Take heed that your heart go to God as well as your mouth. Let not your mouth go any farther than you strive to draw your heart along with it. The lips without the heart argue.

—Discourse on Prayer

Many ask and have not because they ask amiss, and so are never nearer enjoying those things they petition for. It is not to pray at random that will cause God to answer. While prayer is making, God is searching the heart to see from what root and spirit it arises. And he who searches the heart knows the meaning of the Spirit, because he makes intercession for the saints according to the will of God. Without the Spirit, though we have a thousand Common Prayer books, yet we will not know what we should pray for as we ought, being accompanied by those infirmities that make us absolutely incapable of such a work.

—Discourse on Prayer

Prayer is a sincere, sensible, affectionate pouring out of the heart or soul to God through Christ by the strength or assistance of the Spirit. For without a sincere, sensible, affectionate pouring out of the heart to God it is but lip-labor, and if it is not through Christ it falls far short of ever sounding well in the ears of God. *—Discourse on Prayer*

Prayer will make a man cease from sin, or sin will entice a man to cease from prayer.

—Bunyan's Dying Sayings (of Prayer)

He that cannot abide to keep one day holy to God has given sufficient proof that he is an unsanctified man. And, as such, what will he do in heaven, that being the place where a perpetual sabbath is to be kept to God? And for all I know, one reason why one day in seven has been set apart by our Lord unto holy duties for men may be to give them conviction that there is enmity in the hearts of sinners to the God of heaven. For he that hates holiness hates God himself. He pretends to love God, yet loves not a holy day.

—*The Life and Death of Mr. Badman*

Prayer, if the heart is not in it, is like a sound without life. And a heart that is not lifted up of the Spirit will never pray to God.   —*Discourse on Prayer*

God never did account Paul a praying man until he was a convinced and converted man. No more will it be with anyone else.   —*Discourse on Prayer*

There is an exceeding difference between the notion of the flesh and blood, and the revelation of God in heaven; also a great difference between that faith that is feigned, according to man's wisdom, and that which comes by a man's being born of God.

—*Grace Abounding to the Chief of Sinners*

Pray often, for prayer is a shield to the soul, a sacrifice to God, and a scourge for Satan.

—*Bunyan's Dying Sayings (of Prayer)*

He that enters into the house of the Lord is an ascending man, as it is said of Moses that he went up into the mount of God. It is ascending to go into the house of God. The world doesn't believe this. They think it is going downward to go up to the house of God, but they are in a horrible mistake.

—Solomon's Temple Spiritualized

Prayer is one of the first things that proves a man to be a Christian. If it is right it is a prayer which desires God in Christ, for himself and for his holiness, love, wisdom and glory. For right prayer, as it runs on to God through Christ, centers in him and in him alone.

There are two things that provoke to prayer: The one is a detestation of sin and the things of this life; the other is a longing desire after communion with God in a holy and undefiled state and inheritance.

—Discourse on Prayer

I went to seek the Lord, and as I prayed, I cried, and my soul cried to him in these words, with strong cries, "O Lord, I beseech thee, shew me that thou hast loved me with an everlasting love." I had no sooner said it, but with sweetness this returned upon me, as an echo, or sounding again, "I have loved thee with an everlasting love." Now I went to bed in quiet; also when I awaked the next morning, it was fresh upon my soul, and I believed it.

—Grace Abounding to the Chief of Sinners

Chapter Four

SAFE LODGINGS FOR MY SOUL

" . . . your soul lies not only under a special invitation to come, but also under a promise of being accepted and forgiven."

Faith lodges the soul with Christ. "I know (saith Paul) whom I have believed (and to whom I have committed my soul), and am persuaded (I believe it) that he is able to keep that which I have committed unto him against that day" (2 Tim. 1:12). Therefore it was no shame for him to wear a chain for his name and sake. Oh, it is a blessed thing to see, by faith in the Lord Jesus, that we are embarked in the same ship with him. This will help us greatly both to "hope and quietly wait for the salvation of the Lord" (Lam. 3:26). *—Justification by an Imputed Righteousness*

What is faith but a believing, a trusting, a relying act of the soul! What then must it rely upon or trust in? Not in faith itself; that is without Scripture. Not in its works; they are inferior to itself. Besides, this is the way to make even the works of faith the mediator between God and the soul, and so by them thrust Christ out of doors. Therefore faith must trust in Christ. *—Justification by an Imputed Righteousness*

There are three false opinions of God: 1. Some think he is all mercy and no justice, and therefore they may live any way they want. 2. Others think he is all justice and no mercy, and therefore they may as well go on in their sins and be damned as turn and never be the better. 3. Others think he is both justice and mercy, but also think that his justice is such that they can pacify him with their own good works and save themselves with their own right hands.

—Instruction for the Ignorant

Allow yourself by the authority of the Word to be persuaded that the Scripture indeed is the Word of God, and that they therefore must be every one true, pure, and forever settled in heaven.

Conclude, therefore, that the God whose words they are is able to make a reconciliation and a most sweet and harmonious agreement with all the sayings therein, no matter how obscure, cross, dark, or contradictory they seem to you.

—Of the Trinity, and a Christian

Many, yea, most men, believe the Scriptures as they believe a fable, a story, a tale of which there is no certainty! But alas, there are but few that do in deed and in truth believe the Scriptures to be the very word of God. *—The Groans of a Damned Soul*

Be careful that you do not receive this doctrine of justification by faith in notion only lest you bring a just damnation upon your soul by professing yourself to be freed by Christ's blood from the guilt of sin while you still remain a servant to the filth of sin.

For I must tell you that unless you have the true and saving work of the faith and grace of the gospel in your hearts, you will either go on in a legal holiness, according to the tenor of the law, or else, through a notion of the gospel, you will turn the grace of God into wantonness and bring upon your soul double, if not treble, damnation. This is because you would not be content to be damned for your sins against the law but also, in order to make ruin certain for your soul, you would dishonor the gospel and turn the grace of God into licentiousness.

But so that you might be sure to escape these dangerous rocks on the right hand and on the left, see that your faith is such as is spoken of in the Scripture. Be sure that you are not satisfied without that. Have a faith wrought by the mighty operation of God, revealing Christ to you, and in you, as having wholly freed you from your sins by his most precious blood. This faith, if you attain unto it, will so work in your heart that first you will delight in the glory of it, and also you will find an engraving of your heart and soul to Jesus Christ even to the giving up of the whole man to him, to be ruled and governed by him for his glory and your comfort.

—*The Groans of a Damned Soul*

God's people are fruitful in good works according to the proportion of their faith. If they be slender in good works, it is because they are weak in faith. Little faith is like small candles, or weak fire, which though they shine and have heat yet have but dim shining and small heat when compared with bigger candles and greater fire. —*Christian Behavior*

Has he said it, and shall he not do it? Has he spoken, and shall he not bring it to pass? His decrees are composed according to his eternal wisdom, established upon his unchangeable will, governed by his knowledge, prudence, power, justice and mercy, and are brought to conclusion (on his part) in perfect holiness. "He is the Rock, his work is perfect: for all his ways are judgment: a God of truth and without iniquity, just and right is he" (Deut. 32:4).
—*Election and Reprobation*

If your faith is not accompanied by a holy life, you shall be judged a withered branch, a worldling, salt without savor, and as lifeless as sounding brass and a tinkling cymbal.

But, I say, if you walk as becomes one who is saved by grace, then you will witness to every man's conscience that you are a good tree. The ear that hears such a man shall bless him, and the eye that sees him shall bear witness to him. —*Christian Behavior*

For a man to come to Christ for life, though he come to him for nothing else but life, is to give much honor to him. He honors the word of Christ and consents to the truth of it. He honors Christ's person in that he believes that there is life in him, and that he is able to save him from death, hell, the devil, and damnation. He honors him in that he believes that he is authorized by the Father to give life to those who come to him for it. He honors the priesthood of Jesus Christ in that he believes that Christ has more power to save from sin by the sacrifice that he has offered than has all law, devils, death, or sin to condemn. Further, he who comes to Jesus Christ for life takes part with him against sin, and against the ragged and imperfect righteousness of the world.

Wherefore, coming sinner, be content. He who comes to Jesus Christ believes that he is willing to show mercy to and have compassion upon him who comes to him for life. Therefore your soul lies not only under a special invitation to come, but also under a promise of being accepted and forgiven.

—Come, and Welcome, to Jesus Christ

Look before you. Do you see this narrow way? That is the way you must go. It was put up by the patriarchs, prophets, Christ, and his apostles, and it is as straight as a rule can make it. This is the way you must go.

—The Pilgrim's Progress

God's word has two edges; it can cut back-stroke and fore-stroke. If it does you no good, it will do you hurt. It is the savor of life unto life to those that receive it, but of death unto death to them that refuse it.

—The Jerusalem Sinner Saved

Faith reveals the truth of things to the soul: the truth of things as they are, whether they be things that are of this world or of that which is to come; the things and pleasures above, and also those beneath. Faith reveals to the soul the blessedness and goodness and durableness of the one; the vanity, foolishness, and transitoriness of the other.

—Justification by an Imputed Righteousness

If we talk of wisdom, our Jesus is wise. He is wiser than Solomon, wiser than all men, wiser than all angels. He is the wisdom of God.

—Come, and Welcome, to Jesus Christ

I say, if the rich man should say to the poor, "Come to my door, ask at my door, knock at my door, and you shall find and have," would he not be reckoned a free-hearted man? Why, thus does Jesus Christ.

He does not only bid you come but tells you he will heartily do you good. Yea, he will do it with rejoicing.

—Come, and Welcome, to Jesus Christ

Life must be by Jesus Christ so that God may be adored and magnified for finding this way. This is the Lord's doings, that in all things he might be glorified through Jesus Christ.

It must be by Jesus Christ that life might be at God's disposal, for he has great pity for the poor, the lowly, the meek, and the broken in heart.

Life must be in Christ to cut off boasting from the lips of men.

Life must be in Jesus Christ that we might have it upon the easiest terms: to wit, freely, as a gift not as wages. But thanks be to God, it is in Christ. It is laid up in him, and by him to be communicated to sinners upon easy terms, even to receiving, accepting, and embracing with thanksgiving.

Life is in Christ for us that it might not be upon so brittle a foundation, as indeed it would had it been anywhere else. But Christ is a tried stone, a sure foundation, one who will not fail to bear your burden and to receive your soul.

—*Come, and Welcome, to Jesus Christ*

To tell you the truth, I love him because I was by him eased of my burden, and I am weary of my inward sickness. I would prefer to be where I shall die no more, and with the company that shall continually cry, "Holy, holy, holy!"—*The Pilgrim's Progress*

Suppose one man should die quietly, another should die suddenly, and a third should die under great consternation of spirit. No man can judge their eternal condition by the manner of any of these deaths. He who dies quietly, suddenly, or under consternation of spirit, may go to heaven, or may go to hell; no man can tell whether a man goes by the manner of death.

The judgment, therefore, that we make of the eternal condition of man must be gathered from another consideration: Did the man die in his sins? Did he die in unbelief? Did he die before he was born again? If so, then he is gone to the devil and hell, even though he died ever so quietly. Again, was the man a good man? Had he faith and holiness? Was he a lover and a worshipper of God in Christ according to his Word? Then he is gone to God and heaven.

—The Life and Death of Mr. Badman

It must not be supposed that Christ's words are bigger than his worthiness. He is strong to execute his word. He can do as well as speak. He can do "exceeding abundantly above all that we ask or think" (Eph. 3:20).

Do you suppose that the Lord Jesus did not think before he spoke? He speaks in all righteousness, and therefore by his word we are to judge how mighty he is to save.

He spoke in righteousness, in faithfulness, when he began to build this blessed gospel fabric. He first sat down and counted the cost, and knew he was able to finish it!

—Come, and Welcome, to Jesus Christ

Faith and doubting may at the same time have residence in the same soul. "O thou of little faith, wherefore didst thou doubt?" (Matt. 14:31). Jesus did not say, "O thou of no faith," but, "O thou of little faith," because Peter had a little faith in the midst of his many doubts.

The same is true even of many who are coming to Jesus Christ. They come, and fear they do not come, or doubt they come. When they look upon the promise, or a word of encouragement by faith, then they come. But when they look upon themselves, or the difficulties that lie before them, then they doubt. "Bid me come," said Peter. "Come," said Christ. So he went out of the ship to go to Jesus. But his doubt was to go with him upon the water, and there was the trial.

So it is with the poor desiring soul. "Bid me come," says the sinner. "Come," says Christ, "and I will in no wise cast you out" (John 6:37). So he comes. But when he comes upon the water, upon drowning difficulties, if the wind of temptations blow, then the waves of doubts and fears will presently arise. And this coming sinner will begin to sink if he has but little faith.   —*Come, and Welcome, to Jesus Christ*

Oh, the heart-attracting glory that is in Jesus Christ to draw to him those who are given to him of the Father. And the reason why others come not, but perish in their sins, is for lack of a sight of his glory. "If our gospel be hid, it is hid to them that are lost: in whom the god of this world hath blinded the minds of them which believe not, lest the light of the glorious gospel of Christ, who is the image of God, should shine unto them" (2 Cor. 4:3, 4).

There is therefore heart-pulsing glory in Jesus Christ which, when discovered, draws men to him. Indeed, his glory is veiled and cannot be seen, except as revealed by the Father. It is veiled with flesh, with lowliness of descent from the flesh, and with that ignominy and shame that attended him in the flesh. But they who can, in God's light, see through these things, shall see glory in him, yea, such glory as will draw and pull their hearts toward him.

—*Come, and Welcome, to Jesus Christ*

There are times when some graces may be out of use, but there is no time wherein faith can be said to be out of use. Faith always must be exercised.

Faith is the eye, the mouth, the hand—and one of these is in use all day long. Faith is to see, to receive, to work, or to eat—and a Christian should be seeing, or receiving, or working, or feeding all day long. Let it rain, let it blow, let it thunder, let it lightning; a Christian must still believe.

—*The Jerusalem Sinner Saved*

Christ will never lose his sweet scent in the nostrils of his church. He is most sweet now, will be so at death, and sweetest of all when by him we shall enter into that mansion house prepared for us in heaven.
—*Solomon's Temple Spiritualized*

In heaven I hope to see him alive who did hang dead on the cross. And there I hope to be rid of all those things that to this day are in me and an annoyance to me. There, they say, there is no death. And there I shall dwell with such company as I like best.
—*The Pilgrim's Progress*

Will it not be glorious to have this sentence: "Come, ye blessed of my Father, inherit the kingdom prepared for you from the foundation of the world" (Matt. 25:34). Will it not be glorious to enter with the angels and saints into that glorious kingdom? How will it comfort you to see you have not lost that glory, to think that the devil has not got your soul, that your soul should be saved and that not by a little but a great salvation.

Oh, therefore let the saints be joyful in glory; let them triumph over all their enemies. Let them begin to sing about heaven upon earth, about triumph before they come to glory, even when they are in the midst of their enemies. "This honour have all his saints" (Ps. 149:9).
—*The Groans of a Damned Soul*

Friend, you who seek after this world and desire riches, let me ask this question: Would you be content if God should put you off with a portion in this life? Would you be glad to be kept out of heaven with a back well clothed and a belly well filled with the dainties of this world? Would you be glad to have all the good things in your lifetime, to have your heaven to last no longer than while you live in this world? Would you be willing to be deprived of eternal happiness and felicity? If you say no, then have a care of the world and your sins.   —*The Groans of a Damned Soul*

Faith wraps up the soul in the bundle of life with God. It encloses it in the righteousness of Jesus, and presents it so perfect that, whatever Satan can do with all his cunning, he cannot render the soul spotted or wrinkled before the justice of the law. Yea, though the man in his own person and acts is full of sin from top to toe, Jesus Christ covers all. Faith sees it, and holds the soul in its godly sense. Thus therefore the soul, believing, is hid from all the power of the enemy and dwells safely under the dominion of grace.

—*Justification by an Imputed Righteousness*

Chapter Five

LIKE FLOWERS IN A GARDEN

"If you are the children of God, live together lovingly."

hristians are like the several flowers in a garden that have upon each of them the dew of heaven, which being shaken with the wind, they let fall the dew at each other's roots whereby they are jointly nourished and become nourishers of one another.
—*Christian Behavior*

The best way both to provoke ourselves and others to good works is to be often affirming to others the doctrine of justification by grace, and to believe it ourselves. —*Christian Behavior*

The churches should love their pastors, hear their pastors, be ruled by their pastors, and suffer themselves to be watched over and to be exhorted, counselled, and, if need be, reproved and rebuked by their pastors. Let the ministers not sleep, but be watchful and look to the ordinances, to the souls of the saints, and to the gates of the churches. Watchman, Watchman—watch. —*Solomon's Temple Spiritualized*

Christians are strong when united; then they are more able to resist temptation and to succour such as are tempted. When unity and peace are among the churches, then they are like a walled town, and when peace is the church's walls, salvation will be her bulwarks.   —*An Exhortation to Peace and Unity*

Holiness of life is essential to church communion. It seems to be the reason why Christ founded a church in the world, that men might thereby be watched over and kept from falling, and that if any be overtaken with a fault, he that is spiritual might restore him (Gal. 6:1). It appears that an unholy and profane life is inconsistent with Christian religion and society.   —*An Exhortation to Peace and Unity*

Oh, my soul, this is not the place of despair. This is not the time to despair. As long as my eyes can find a promise in the Bible, as long as there is the least mention of grace, as long as there is a moment left to me of breath or life in this world, so long will I wait or look for mercy, so long will I fight against unbelief and despair.   —*The Jerusalem Sinner Saved*

Peace is to Christians as great rivers are to some cities: natural fortifications to make those places impregnable. But when by the subtlety of an adversary or the folly of the citizen these waters come to be divided into little petty rivulets, how soon are they assailed and taken? Thus it fares with churches. When once the devil or their own folly divides them, they will be so far from resisting him that they will soon be subjected by him. *—An Exhortation to Peace and Unity*

It is common with wicked men to hate God's servants while alive and to commend them when they are dead. *—The Life and Death of Mr. Badman*

There is little faithful dealing with men nowadays, and that makes religion to stink in the nostrils of many. For there are these talkative fools whose religion is only in words, but who are debauched and vain in their manner of living, that being admitted into the fellowship of the godly they do puzzle the world, blemish Christianity, and grieve the sincere.
—The Pilgrim's Progress

The Holy Ghost never intended that men who have gifts and abilities should bury them in the earth, but rather did command and stir up such to the exercise of their gifts, and also did commend those that were apt and ready so to do.
—Grace Abounding to the Chief of Sinners

Forsake not the public worship of God lest God forsake you, not only in public but in private.

—Bunyan's Dying Sayings (of the Lord's Day,
Sermons, and Week-Days)

In the church be careful to serve God, for you are in his eyes and not in man's.

—Bunyan's Dying Sayings (of the Lord's Day,
Sermons, and Week-Days)

If you are the king's children, live like the king's children. If you are risen with Christ, set your affection on things above, not on things on the earth (Col. 3:1, 2). When you come together, talk of what your Father promised you. You should all love your Father's will, and be contented and pleased with the exercises with which you meet in the world. If you are the children of God, live together lovingly. If the world quarrels with you, it is no matter, but it is sad if you quarrel together. If quarreling is among you, it is a sign of ill breeding; it is according to no rules you have in the Word of God. Do you see a soul that has the image of God in him? Love him, love him. Say, this man and I must go to heaven one day. Serve one another, do good for one another, and if any wrong you, pray to God to right you; and love the brotherhood. *—Bunyan's Last Sermon*

One morning as I was at prayer and trembling under the fear that no word of God could help me, that piece of a sentence darted in upon me: "My grace is sufficient" (2 Cor. 12:9). At this I thought I felt some hope. Oh, how great a thing it is for God to send his word! For about a fortnight before I was looking on this very place, and at that time I thought it could not comfort my soul. Therefore I threw down my book in a pet. Then I thought it was not large enough for me, but now it is as if it has arms of grace so wide that it can not only enclose me but many more beside.   —*Grace Abounding to the Chief of Sinners*

Chapter Six

HEDGES HAVE EYES . . . AND LITTLE PITCHERS, EARS

" . . . children make a greater inspection into the lives of fathers, masters, etc., than ofttimes they are aware of."

If the master has one guise for abroad and another for home; that is, if his religion hangs in his house as his cloak does, and he be seldom in it except he be abroad, this young beginner will take notice and stumble. We say, hedges have eyes, and little pitchers have ears; and indeed, children make a greater inspection into the lives of fathers, masters, etc., than ofttimes they are aware of.

—*The Life and Death of Mr. Badman*

The children of godly parents are the children of many prayers. They are prayed for before and prayed for after they are born. The prayers of a godly father and a godly mother do much.

—*The Life and Death of Mr. Badman*

Take heed that the misdeeds for which you correct your children are not learned from you. Many children learn from their parents the wickedness for which they are beaten and chastised.

Take heed that you do not smile to encourage your children in small faults lest your attitude toward them be an encouragement for them to commit greater.

Take heed that you do not use unsavory and unseemly words in chastising them. This is devilish.

Take heed that you do not use many chiding and threatening words mixed with lightness and laughter; this will burden them. Be sure that your speech is pertinent to them, with all gravity.

—Christian Behavior

Children have the benefit of a godly life set before them doctrinally by their parents, and that doctrine is backed with a godly and holy example. These are very great advantages.

—The Life and Death of Mr. Badman

Be such a husband to your believing wife that she may say, "God has not only given me a husband, but such a husband as preaches to me every day the way of Christ to his church." *—Christian Behavior*

Oh, how little sense of the worth of souls is there in the hearts of some husbands, as is manifest by their unchristian manner to and before their wives!

—Christian Behavior

It is too much the custom of young people now to think themselves wise enough to make their own choices, and that they need not ask counsel of those who are older and wiser than they. This is a great fault with them, and many have paid dearly for it.

—The Life and Death of Mr. Badman

Children, when little, how they do delight us!
When they grow bigger, they begin to fright us.
Their sinful nature prompts them to rebel,
And to delight in paths that lead to hell.
Their parents' love and care they overlook
As if relation had them quite forsook.
They take the counsels of the wanton, rather
Than the most grave instructions of a father.
They reckon parents ought to do for them,
Tho' they the first commandment do condemn.
They snap and snarl if parents them control,
Altho' in things most hurtful to the soul
They reckon they are masters, and that we
Who parents are, should to them subject be!

—Upon the Disobedient Child

I remember that I heard of a good woman who had a bad and ungodly son. And she prayed for him, counselled him, and carried it motherly to him, for several years together, but still he remained bad. At last, after she had been at prayer for his conversion, she came to him and began again to admonish him. "Son," said she, "you have been, and are, a wicked child. You have cost me many a prayer and tear, and yet you remain wicked. Well, I have done my duty; I have done what I can to save you. Now I am satisfied that if I shall see you damned at the day of judgment, I shall be so far off from being grieved for you that I shall rejoice to hear the sentence of your damnation at that day."

And it converted him.

—The Life and Death of Mr. Badman

Isaac was so holy before his children that when Jacob remembered God he remembered that God was the fear of his father Isaac.

Ah, when children can think of their parents and bless God for that instruction and good they have received from them, this is not only profitable for children, but honorable and comfortable to parents.

—Christian Behavior

Chapter Seven

THE BEST DISCOVERY OF OURSELVES

"Oh, consider, I say, consider, and do not put off the offering of the grace of our Lord Jesus Christ . . . "

The death of Christ gives us the best discovery of ourselves: the condition we were in that nothing but that could help, and the clear discovery of the dreadful nature of our sins. For if sin is so dreadful a thing as to wring the heart of the Son of God, how shall a poor wretched sinner be able to bear it?

—Bunyan's Dying Sayings (of Sin)

Christ's church is a hospital of sick, wounded, and afflicted people. Even when he was in the world, the afflicted and distressed set the highest price upon Jesus Christ. Why? Because they were sick, and he was the physician. And thus it is now. Christ is offered to the world to be the righteousness and life of sinners. But no man will regard him save he who sees his own pollution, he who sees he cannot answer the demands of the law, he who sees himself from top to toe polluted. He is the man who must die in despair and be damned, or trust in Jesus Christ for life.

—Justification by an Imputed Righteousness

Some count him a kind of heartless God who
will neither do evil nor good. Some count him a kind
of an ignorant and blind God who can neither know
nor see through the clouds. Some count him an incon-
siderate God who is not worth enjoying if it must mean
the loss of this world and their lusts. Moreover, some
think God to be altogether one such as themselves,
one that has as little hatred of sin as themselves and
as little love of holiness as themselves.

—Instruction for the Ignorant

I never had in all my life so great an inlet into
the Word of God as now. Those Scriptures in which
I saw nothing before are made in this place and state
to shine upon me. Jesus Christ also was never more
real and apparent than now. Here I have seen and
felt him indeed.   *—To the Chief of Sinners*

Tell me, is it not better to leave sin and close
in with Christ Jesus, notwithstanding that reproach you
shall meet for so doing, than to live a little while in
this world in pleasures and feeding your lusts, in ne-
glecting the welfare of your soul and refusing to be
justified by Jesus, and in a moment to drop down to
hell and cry? Oh, consider, I say, consider, and do
not put off the offering of the grace of our Lord Jesus
Christ lest you lift up your eyes in hell and cry for
anguish of spirit.   *—The Groans of a Damned Soul*

What ails this fly who desperately enters
A combat with the candle? Will she venture
To clash with light? Away, you silly fly;
Thus doing you will burn your wings and die.

But 'tis a folly here advice to give;
She'll kill the candle or she will not live.
Slap, says she at it; then she makes retreat,
Then wheels about and does her blows repeat.
But now, behold; the candle takes the fly
And holds her till she does by burning die.

This candle is an emblem of that light
Our gospel gives in this our darksome night.
The fly a lively picture is of those
That hate and do this gospel light oppose.
At last the gospel does become their snare,
And them with burning hands in pieces tear.
                    —*Of the Fly and the Candle*

Have you no reason? Can you not so much as once
think soberly of your dying hour, or where your sinful
life will drive you then? Have you no conscience?
Or, having one, is it rocked so fast asleep by sin or
made so weary with an unsuccessful calling to you
that it is laid down and cares for you no more? Poor
man! Your state is to be lamented.
                    —*The Jerusalem Sinner Saved*

There is no good in this life but what is mingled with some evil. Honors perplex, riches disquiet, and pleasures ruin health. But in heaven we shall find blessings in their purity, without any ingredient to embitter, with everything to sweeten them.

—*Bunyan's Dying Sayings (of the Joys of Heaven)*

God doth not require self-denial as the means to obtain salvation, but has laid it down as a proof of the truth of a man's affections to God and Christ. Self-denial is one of the distinguishing characters by which true Christians are manifested from the feigned ones. For those who are feigned flatter God with their mouths, but their hearts seek themselves. But the sincere, for the love that he has toward Christ, forsakes all that he has for his sake.   —*Instruction for the Ignorant*

He that is down needs fear no fall;
    He that is low, no pride.
He that is humble ever shall
    Have God to be his guide.
I am content with what I have,
    Little be it or much:
And, Lord, contentment still I crave,
    Because thou savest such.
Fulness to such a burden is
    That go on pilgrimage:
Here little, and hereafter bliss,
    Is best from age to age.
        —*The Pilgrim's Progress, Part II*

Man's like a candle in a candlestick,
Made up of tallow and a little wick;
For what the candle is before 'tis lighted,
Just such be they who are in sin benighted.
Nor can a man his soul with grace inspire
More than the candles set themselves on fire.

Candles receive their light from what they are not;
Men grace from him for whom at first they care not.

We manage candles when they take the fire;
God men, when he with grace doth them inspire.

And biggest candles give the better light,
As grace in biggest sinners shines most bright.

The candle shines to make another see;
A saint unto his neighbor light should be.

The blinking candle we do much despise;
Saints dim of light are high in no man's eyes.

—Meditations Upon a Candle

Methinks I see a sight most excellent;
All sorts of birds fly in the firmament:
Some great, some small, all of a divers kind;
Mine eye affecting, pleasant to my mind.
Look how they wing along the wholesome air,
Above the world of worldlings and their care.
And as they divers are in bulk and hue,
So are they in their ways of flying too.
So many birds, so many various things
Swim in the element upon their wings.

Comparison

These birds are emblems of those men that shall
E'er long possess the heavens, their all in all.
They each are of a diff'rent shape and kind;
To teach, we of all nations there shall find.
They are some great, some little as we see,
To show some great, some small, in glory be.
Their flying diversity, as we behold,
Do show saints joys will there be manifold.
Some glide, some mount, some flutter, and some do
In a mixt way of flying glory too,
To show that each shall to his full content
Be happy in that heav'nly firmament.

—Of Fowls Flying in the Air

The question is not what men themselves believe
concerning their sin but what God's word says about
it.   *—The Life and Death of Mr. Badman*

I observe two things very odious in many professors of faith: the one is a head-strong and stiff-necked spirit that will have its own way, and the other is a great deal of tattling and talk about religion, but very little of those Christian deeds that carry in them the cross of a Christian in the doing thereof, and profit to my neighbor.

When I say a head-strong and stiff-necked spirit, I mean they are for pleasing themselves and their own fancies in things of no weight, though their so doing is as the very slaughter-knife to the weak conscience of a brother or neighbor. Now this is base. A Christian in all things should be full of self-denial, and seek to please others rather than himself.

And the second is as bad; to wit, when professors of faith are great prattlers and talkers and disputers, but do little of anything that bespeaks love to the poor or self-denial in outward things. Some people think religion is made up of words, a very wide mistake. Words without deeds is but a half-faced religion: "Pure religion and undefiled before God and the Father is this, To visit the fatherless and widows in their affliction, and to keep (thyself) unspotted from the world" (James 1:27). Again, "If a brother or a sister be naked and destitute of daily food, and one of you say unto them, Depart in peace, be warmed and filled (which are very fine words); notwithstanding ye give them not those things that are needful to the body; what doth it profit?" (James 2:15, 16). —*Christian Behavior*

I thought it impossible that ever I should attain to so much godliness of heart as to thank God that he had made me a man. Man indeed is the most noble by creation of all creatures in the visible world, but by sin he has made himself the most ignoble. The beasts, birds, fishes, etc., I blessed their condition for they had not a sinful nature; they were not obnoxious to the wrath of God; they were not to go to hellfire after death. I could therefore have rejoiced had my condition been as any of theirs.

In this condition I went a great while. But when the comforting time was come, I heard one preach a sermon on these words in the Song, "Behold, thou art fair, my love; behold, thou art fair." But I got nothing from what he said at present, only when he came to the application. This was the word he said: "If it be so that the saved soul is Christ's love when under temptation and destruction, then, poor tempted soul, when you are assaulted and afflicted with temptations and the hidings of his face, yet still think on those two words, *my love.*"

—Grace Abounding to the Chief of Sinners

Men who are wicked themselves greatly hate it in others. Yes, they condemn that in another which they either have or do allow in themselves. The time will come when that very sentence that has gone out of their own mouths against the sins of others, when they live and take pleasure in the same, shall return with violence upon their own heads.

—The Life and Death of Mr. Badman

The drunkard loves the sin, but loves not to be called a drunkard. The thief loves to steal, but cannot abide to be called a thief. They love the vice but care not to bear its name.

—The Life and Death of Mr. Badman

I once talked with a maid by way of reproof about her gaudy garments. But she told me, "The tailor made it so." Alas! Poor proud girl. She gave the orders to the tailor. Many make parents and husbands and tailors, etc., blind. But their naughty hearts and their giving way is the original cause of all these evils.

—The Life and Death of Mr. Badman

I think it is one of the most senseless and ridiculous things in the world that a man should be proud of that which is given to him to cover the shame of his nakedness.

—The Life and Death of Mr. Badman

The water is the fish's element;
Leave her there, and she will be content.
So will he who in the path of life does plod.
Take all, says he, but let me have my God.

The water is the fish's element;
Her sportings there to her are excellent.
So is God's service unto holy men;
They are not in their element till then.

—Upon the Fish in the Water

Chapter Eight

AN EMPTY BELLY—A FATTED CALF

"No sins of the coming sinner, nor the length of the time that he has abode in them, shall prevail with Jesus Christ to reject him."

The prodigal, when coming home to his father, was clothed with nothing but rags and was tormented with an empty belly. But when he was come, the best robe was brought out, also the gold ring and the shoes. Yea, they were put upon him, to his great rejoicing. The fatted calf was killed for him; the music was struck up to make him merry. And thus also the Father himself sang of him. "This my son was dead, and is alive again; he was lost, and is found" (Luke 15:24).

In a word, he that is come to Christ, his groans and tears, his doubts and fears are turned into songs and praises. For he has now received the atonement, and the earnest of his inheritance.

—Come, and Welcome, to Jesus Christ

I began to give place to the word which with power did over and over make this joyful sound within my soul: "Thou art my love, thou art my love, and nothing shall separate thee from my love." I was now so taken with the love and mercy of God that I could not tell how to contain till I got home.

—Grace Abounding to the Chief of Sinners

This word "in no wise" cuts the throat of all objections. It was dropped by the Lord Jesus for that very end, to help the faith that is mixed with unbelief.

Neither can any objection be made upon an unworthiness that this promise will not assail.

But I am a great sinner, you say.

I will in no wise cast out, says Christ.

But I am an old sinner, you say.

I will in no wise cast out, says Christ.

But I am a hard-hearted sinner, you say.

I will in no wise cast out, says Christ.

But I am a backsliding sinner, you say.

I will in no wise cast out, says Christ.

But I have served Satan all my days, you say.

I will in no wise cast out, says Christ.

But I have sinned against light, you say.

I will in no wise cast out, says Christ.

But I have sinned against mercy, you say.

I will in no wise cast out, says Christ.

But I have no good thing to bring with me, you say.

I will in no wise cast out, says Christ (John 6:37).

     —Come, and Welcome, to Jesus Christ

It is not the over-heavy load of sin, but the discovery of mercy; not the roaring of the devil, but the drawing of the Father, that makes a man come to Jesus Christ.   *—Come, and Welcome, to Jesus Christ*

Faith is so great an artist in arguing and reasoning with the soul that it will bring over the hardest heart with which it has to deal. It will bring to my remembrance both my vileness against God and his goodness toward me; it will show me that though I do not deserve to breathe in the air, yet God will have me an heir of glory.   —*Christian Behavior*

As Jesus Christ has his eye upon and his heart open, nothing shall alienate his heart from receiving the coming sinner. No sins of the coming sinner, nor the length of the time that he has abode in them, shall prevail with Jesus Christ to reject him. Coming sinner, you are coming to a loving Lord Jesus.
                —*Come, and Welcome, to Jesus Christ*

He ran till he came to a place somewhat ascending. Upon that place stood a cross, and a little below, in the bottom, a sepulchre. I saw that just as Christian came to the cross, his burden loosed from off his shoulders, fell from off his back, and began to tumble till it came to the mouth of the sepulchre. It fell in, and I saw it no more.   —*The Pilgrim's Progress*

O hard-hearted and deplorable town of Mansoul, how long will you love your sinful simplicity and delight in your scorning? Do you yet despise the offers of peace and deliverance? Do you yet refuse the golden offers of Shaddai, and trust to the lies and falsehoods of Diabolus? Do you think when Shaddai conquers you that the remembrance of this your manner towards him will yield you peace and comfort, or that by ruffling language you can make him afraid as a grasshopper? Does he entreat you for fear of you? Do you think you are stronger than he? Look to the heavens and behold the stars: how high are they? Can you stop the sun from running its course and hinder the moon from giving her light? Can you call for the waters of the sea and cause them to cover the face of the ground? Can you behold everyone that is proud and abase him, and bind their faces in secret? Yet these are some of the works of our King in whose name this day we come up unto you that you may be brought under his authority. *—The Holy War*

Get your heart warmed with the sweet promise of Christ's acceptance, and that will make you hasten unto him. Discouraging thoughts are like cold water; they benumb the senses and make us go ungainly about our business. But the sweet and warm embers of promise are like the comfortable beams of the sun which enliven and refresh. You see how little the bee and the fly do play in the air in winter. Why? Because the cold hinders them from doing it. But when the wind and sun is warm, who are so busy as they?

—Come, and Welcome, to Jesus Christ

Jesus to whom you are coming is lowly in heart; he despises not any. It is not your outward meanness nor your inward weakness, it is not because you are poor, or base, or deformed, or a fool, that he will despise you. He has chosen the foolish, the base and despised things of this world to confound the wise and mighty. He will bow his ear to your stammering prayers, he will pick out the meaning of your inexpressible groans, he will respect your weakest offering if there be in it your heart. Now is not this a blessed Christ?   —*Come, and Welcome, to Jesus Christ*

A man is a son only as he is begotten and born of God to himself, and a servant as he is gifted for work in the house of his father. And though it is true that the servant may be a son, yet he is not a son because he is a servant. Nor does it follow that because all sons may be servants therefore all servants are sons. No, all the servants of God are not sons. Therefore, when time shall come, he that is only a servant here shall certainly be put out of the house, even out of that house that he himself did help to build.

The sum then is that a man may be a servant and a son: a servant as he is employed by Christ in this house for the good of others, and a son as he is a partaker of the grace of adoption. But all servants are not sons. Let this be for a caution and a call to ministers to do all acts of service for God in his house with reverence and godly fear. And with all humility let us desire to be partakers ourselves of that grace which we preach to others.   —*Solomon's Temple Spiritualized*

One day I was very sad, I think sadder than at any time of my life. This sadness was through a fresh sight of the greatness and vileness of my sins. As I was then looking for nothing but hell, and the everlasting damnation of my soul, suddenly I saw the Lord Jesus look down from heaven upon me saying, "Believe on the Lord Jesus Christ, and thou shalt be saved" (Acts 16:31).

But I replied, "Lord, I am a great, a very great sinner."

He answered, "My grace is sufficient for thee."

Then I said, "But, Lord, what is believing?" And then I saw from that saying, "He that cometh to me shall never hunger; and he that believeth on me shall never thirst" (John 6:35), that believing and coming was all one, and he who came, that is, ran out in his heart and affection after salvation by Christ, he indeed believed in Christ.   —*The Pilgrim's Progress*

O Lord Jesus, what a load you did carry! What a burden you did bear of the sins of the world and the wrath of God! Not only did you bleed at nose and mouth with the pressure that lay upon you, but you were so pressed, so loaded, that the pure blood gushed through the flesh and skin, and so ran trickling down to the ground.

Can you read this, O thou wicked sinner, and yet go on in sin? Can you think of this and defer repentance one hour longer? O heart of flint, yea, harder! O miserable wretch! What place in hell will be hot enough for you to have your soul put into if you will persist or still go on to add iniquity to iniquity.

—*The Groans of a Damned Soul*

After I had considered the sins of the saints in particular, and found mine went beyond them, I began to think with myself. I set this case: should I put all their sins together and mine alone against them, might I not find encouragement? For if mine though bigger than anyone should be but equal to all, then there is hope; for that blood that has virtue enough in it to wash away theirs has virtue enough in it to wash away mine. —*Grace Abounding to the Chief of Sinners*

Until grace displays itself and overcomes the soul with its glory, it is altogether without heart to oppose sin. Besides, if sin is Satan's cord by which the soul lies bound, how should it make resistance before it is loosed from that infirmity? Nor will any who knows either reason or grace believe that such a man can be a living monument of grace who is a slave to his own corruption. —*The Pilgrim's Progress, Part II*

The Merciful One has sent me to tell you that he is a God ready to forgive, and that he takes delight to multiply the pardon of offences. He also would have you know that he invites you to come into his presence, to his table, and that he will feed you with the fat of his house. —*The Pilgrim's Progress, Part II*

Learn to judge the largeness of God's heart and of the heart of his Son Jesus Christ by the word. Judge not thereof by feeling, nor by the reports of the conscience. Conscience is oftentimes befooled and made to go quiet beside the word.

—The Jerusalem Sinner Saved

Do you love your own soul? Then pray to Jesus Christ for an awakened heart, for a heart so awakened with all the things of another world that you may be allured to Jesus Christ. *—The Strait Gate*

Ask your heart: If this morning you were to die, are you ready to die or no?

—Instruction for the Ignorant

The end of affliction is the discovery of sin, and that brings us to a Savior. Let us therefore with the prodigal return unto him, and we shall find ease and rest.

—Bunyan's Dying Sayings (of Repentance and Coming to Christ)

The egg's no chick by falling from the hen;
Nor man a Christian till he's born again.

The egg is first contained within the shell;
Men, before grace, in sins and darkness dwell.
The egg, when laid, by warmth is made a chicken;
And Christ, by grace, the dead-in-sin does quicken.
The chick at first is in the cell confined;
So heaven born souls are in the flesh detained.
The shell then breaks; the chick's at liberty.
The flesh falls off; the soul mounts up on high.
But both do not enjoy the selfsame plight:
The soul is safe; the chick now fears the kite.

—Meditations Upon an Egg

Some men are blood-red sinners, crimson sinners, sinners of a double dye, dipped and dipped again before they come to Jesus Christ. Are you who reads these lines such a one? Speak out man. Are you such a one? And are you now coming to Jesus Christ for the mercy of justification that you might be cleansed in his blood and be covered with his righteousness? Fear not, for he will in no wise cast you out. "Come now," says the Lord, "and let us reason together; though your sins be as scarlet, they shall be as white as snow; though they be red like crimson, they shall be as wool" (Isa. 1:18).

—Come, and Welcome, to Jesus Christ

If a man should see a pearl worth a hundred pounds lying in a ditch, yet did not understand its value, he would lightly pass it by. But if he once got the knowledge of its worth, he would venture up to the neck for it. So it is with souls concerning the things of God. If a man once gets an understanding of their worth, then his heart, indeed the very strength of his soul, runs after them, and he will never leave crying till he has them.   *—Discourse on Prayer*

Chapter Nine

A DAGGER IN ITS SLEEVE

"They will cry to think that they had been so foolish as to follow their pleasures when others were following Christ."

Fools make a mock of sin; they will not believe
It carries such a dagger in its sleeve.
How can it be, they say, that such a thing
So full of sweetness should ever wear a sting?
They know not that it is the very spell
Of Sin, to make men laugh themselves to hell.
                    —*A Caution to Stir Up to Watch Against Sin*

Only faith knows how to deal with mercy. Therefore, do not put anything in its place. I have observed
that just as there are herbs and flowers in our gardens
so there are counterfeits in the field, only they are
wild ones. There is faith, and wild faith. I call it wild
faith because God never placed it in his garden, his
church; it is only to be found in the field, the world.
I also call it wild faith because it only grows up and
is nourished where other wild notions abound.
                              —*The Jerusalem Sinner Saved*

There is never a poor soul who is going to heaven but the devil, the law, sin, death, and hell will go after him. "Your adversary, the devil, as a roaring lion, walketh about, seeking whom he may devour" (1 Pet. 5:8). I assure you, the devil is nimble, he can run apace, he is light of foot. He has overtaken many; he has turned up their heels and has given them an everlasting fall.

Hell has a wide mouth; it can stretch itself farther than you are aware of.   *—The Heavenly Footman*

Why should Satan molest those whose ways he knows will bring them to him? And who thinks that he will be quiet when men take the right course to escape his hellish snares? This is the reason why the truly humble person is opposed, while the presumptuous ones go on by wind and tide. The truly humble Satan hates, but he laughs to see the foolery of the other.

—The Jerusalem Sinner Saved

From God he's a backslider;
Of ways, he loves the wider;
With wickedness a sider;
More venom than a spider.

In sin he's a confider,
A make-bate and divider.
Blind reason is his guider;
The devil is his rider.

—Of Man by Nature

If your heart at any time tempts you to sin against God, cry out, "No, for then I must go to hell and lie there forever." If the drunkards, swearers, liars and hypocrites would ponder this doctrine, it would make them tremble when they think of sinning. But, poor souls, they make a mock of sin and play with it as a child plays with a rattle.

But the time is coming when these rattles which they play with now will make such a noise in their ears and consciences that even if all the devils in hell were yelling at their heels, the noise would not be comparable to it. Friend, your sins, as so many blood hounds, will first hunt you out, then take you and bind you and hold you down forever. They will gnaw you as if you had a nest of poisonous serpents in your bowels. And this will not be for a time, but forever, forever, forever.   —*The Groans of a Damned Soul*

Sin turns all God's grace into wantonness. It is the dare of his justice, the rape of his mercy, the jeer of his patience, the slight of his power, and the contempt of his love.   —*Bunyan's Dying Sayings (of Sin)*

Sins go not alone, but follow one the other as do the links of a chain.

—*The Life and Death of Mr. Badman*

Sin is that beastly thing that will defile
Soul, body, name, and fame in little while.
'Twill make him who some time God's was,
Look like the devil, love and plead his cause.
Like to the plague, poison, or leprosy,
Defile it will, and infect contagiously.
  Wherefore beware, against it shut the door.
  If not, it will defile thee more and more.
        —*A Caution to Stir Up to Watch Against Sin*

Ah, mind, why did you do those things
    That now do work my woe?
Ah, will, why were you thus inclined
    Me ever to undo?
My senses, how were you beguiled
    When you said sin was good!
It has in all parts me defiled,
    And drowned me like a flood.
        Serious Meditations Upon the Four Last Things
            (of Hell, and the Estate of Those that Perish)

I am a spider—
    I hide myself when I for flies do wait;
So does the devil when he lays his bait.
If I do fear the losing of my prey,
I stir me, and more snares upon her lay.
This way and that her wings and legs I tie,
That sure as she is caught, so she must die.
But if I see she's like to get away,
Then with my venom I her journey stay.
All which my ways the devil imitates
To catch men, 'cause he their salvation hates.
        —*The Sinner and the Spider*

Hell would be a kind of paradise if it were no worse
than the worst of this world.
—*Bunyan's Dying Sayings (of the Torments of Hell)*

I cannot help but think that it is a great judgment
of God for a man to be given up to the company of
vile men, for what are such but the devil's decoys,
even those by whom he draws the simple into his net.
A whoremaster, a drunkard, a thief—what are they
but the devil's baits by which he catches others?
—*The Life and Death of Mr. Badman*

What judgment more dreadful can a fool be given
up to than to be delivered into the hands of men who
have skill to do nothing but to ripen sin and hasten
its finishing unto damnation?

But such men do not believe that to be given up
of God is in judgment and anger; they rather take
it to be their liberty and do count it their happiness.
They are glad that their cord is loosed and that the
reins are on their necks. They are glad that they may
sin without control and that they may choose such companions as can make them more expert in an evil way.

Their judgment is therefore so much the greater,
because thereto is added blindness of mind and hard-
ness of heart. They are turned to the way of death.
—*The Life and Death of Mr. Badman*

Doubters are such as have their name from their nature. Their nature is to put a question upon every one of the truths of Emmanuel, and their country is called the Land of Doubting. These that came with Diabolus to ruin the town of Mansoul are the natives of that country.
—*The Holy War*

The man who dies with a life full of sin and with a heart void of repentance, although he should die of the most golden disease (if there were any that might be so called), I warrant that his name shall be abhorred in heaven and earth.
—*The Life and Death of Mr. Badman*

Sin will at first, just like a beggar, crave
One penny, or one halfpenny to have.
But if you grant its first suit, 'twill aspire
From pence to pounds, and still will mount up higher
To the whole soul. But if it makes its moan,
Then say, here is not for you; get you gone.
For if you give it entrance at the door,
It will come in, and may go out no more.
—*A Caution to Stir Up to Watch Against Sin*

It was my delight to be taken captive by the devil at his will, being filled with all unrighteousness. From a child I had but few equals, both for cursing, swearing, lying, and blaspheming the holy name of God.

Yea, so settled and rooted was I in these things that they became second nature to me.

—*Grace Abounding to the Chief of Sinners*

Sin, where it reigns, is a mortal enemy to the soul. It blinds the eyes, holds the hands, ties the legs, stops the ears, and makes the heart implacable to resist the Savior of souls. —*Election and Reprobation*

I am persuaded that many think that to swear is a thing that does bravely become them; that it is the best way for a man, when he would put authority or terror to his words, to stuff them full of the sin of swearing. Otherwise, men would not belch out their blasphemous oaths as they do. They take pride in it; they think that to swear is gentleman-like. And having once accustomed themselves to it, they hardly leave it all the days of their lives.

—*The Life and Death of Mr. Badman*

O what a condition will you sail into when you depart this world! If you depart unconverted and not born again, you had better have been smothered the first hour you were born. You had better have been made a dog, a toad, a serpent, any other creature in the world, than to die unconverted.

Here then, before we go any further, you may see that it is not without good ground that these words are spoken by our Lord that when any of the ungodly depart into hell, they will cry.

Cry? Why so?

They will cry to think that they are cut off from the land of the living, never more to have any footing therein.

They will cry to think that the gospel of Christ had been so often offered to them and yet they are not profited by it.

They will cry to think that now, though they would willingly repent and be saved, they are past all recovery.

They will cry to think that they had been so foolish as to follow their pleasures when others were following Christ.

They will cry to think that they must be separated from God, Christ, and the kingdom of heaven forever.

They will cry to think that their crying will now do them no good.

They will cry to think that at the day of judgment they must stand at the left hand of Christ among an innumerable company of damned ones.

They will cry to think that Lazarus, whom once they slighted, is one of them that sits down with Christ to judge, together with Christ to pass a sentence of condemnation on their souls for ever.

They will cry to think that, when the judgment is over and others are taken into the everlasting kingdom of glory, they must depart into that dungeon of darkness where they shall be tormented so long as eternity lasts, without the least intermission or ease.

—The Groans of a Damned Soul

Sin pulled angels out of heaven, pulls men down to hell, and overthrows kingdoms. Who that sees a house on fire will not give the alarm to them that dwell within? Who that sees the land invaded will not set the beacons aflame? Who that sees the devils as roaring lions, continually devouring souls, will not make an outcry? But above all, when we see sin, sinful sin, swallowing up a nation, sinking a nation, and bringing its inhabitants to temporal, spiritual, and eternal ruin, shall we not cry out?   *—The Author to the Reader*

In those days the thoughts of religion were very grievous to me; I could neither endure it myself nor that any other should, so when I saw some read in those books that concerned Christian piety, it would be a prison to me. Then I said unto God, "Depart from me, for I desire not the knowledge of your ways." I was now void of all good consideration; heaven and hell were both out of sight and mind. And as for saving and damning, they were least in my thoughts.

But this I well remember, that though I could myself sin with the greatest delight and ease, and also take pleasure in the vileness of my companions, yet, even then, if I at any time saw wicked things by those who professed goodness, it would make my spirit tremble.

—Grace Abounding to the Chief of Sinners

A lie is a brat of hell. It cannot be in the heart before the person has committed a kind of spiritual adultery with the devil. That soul, therefore, that tells a known lie has conceived it by lying with the devil, the father of lies. For a lie has only one father and mother, the devil and the heart. A liar is wedded to the devil himself. —*The Life and Death of Mr. Badman*

The original fountain of pride is the heart, for out of the heart comes pride. This pride of heart tempts men, and by its deceits overcomes them. Yea, it puts a bewitching virtue into their peacock's feathers, and they are swallowed up by their vanity.
—*The Life and Death of Mr. Badman*

To swear is to call God to witness. And to swear a lie is to call God to witness that the lie is true. This puts the highest afront upon the holiness and righteousness of God. Therefore, his wrath must sweep them away. This kind of swearing is put in with lying, and killing, and stealing, and committing adultery, and must not go unpunished.
—*The Life and Death of Mr. Badman*

Man is God's image, and to curse wickedly the image of God is to curse God himself. Therefore, when men wickedly swear, they rend and tear God's name, and make him the avoucher and approver of all their wickedness. So he that curses and condemns his neighbor, curses and condemns and wishes evil to the image of God. He consequently judges and condemns himself.
—*The Life and Death of Mr. Badman*

Envy is so rank and strong that if it at any
time turns its head against a man, it would hardly ever
be pulled in again. Envy would watch over that man
to do him mischief, as the cat watches the mouse to
destroy it. Yea, he would wait seven years if he could
have an opportunity to hurt him, and when he had it,
he would make him feel the weight of his envy.

Envy is a devilish thing, for the foulness of it is
reckoned among the foulest villanies that there are:
adultery, murder, drunkenness, revellings, witchcrafts,
heresies, seditions, etc. Yes, it is so malignant a corruption that it rots the very bones of him in whom
it dwells.   —*The Life and Death of Mr. Badman*

We count the "damn me" blades to be great
swearers. But when in their hellish fury they say, "God
damn me," "God perish me," or the like, they curse
themselves with a wish that damnation might light upon
themselves. In a little time they will see that wish and
curse of theirs accomplished upon them, even in hell
fire, if they do not repent of their sins.
                    —*The Life and Death of Mr. Badman*

The prisoner who is to die at the gallows for his wickedness must first have his irons knocked off his legs. So he seems to go most at liberty when indeed he is going to be executed for his transgressions. Wicked men also have no bands in their death; they seem to be more at liberty when they are even at the wind-up of their sinful lives than at any time besides.

Hence you shall hear them boast of their faith and hope in God's mercy when they lie upon their death beds. Yea, you shall hear them speak as confidently of their salvation as if they had served God all their days. The truth is, their boasting is because they have no bands in their death.

—The Life and Death of Mr. Badman

Chapter Ten

THE CROWN AT THE END OF THE RACE

"He alone is able to give them all this to the fulfilling of their joy."

Arise, man, be slothful no longer. Set foot and heart and all into the way of God, and run; the crown is at the end of the race. There also stands the loving forerunner, even Jesus, who has prepared heavenly provision to make your soul welcome; and he will give it to you with a more willing heart than you could ever desire of him.　　　　*—An Epistle*

A man who is a teacher may himself learn from another who teaches. Every man who has received a gift from God may dispense it that others may be comforted. And when he has done that, he may hear and learn and be comforted himself by others in return.
　　　　　　　　—Imprisonment of John Bunyan

Oh, my Mansoul! I have lived, I have died; I live, and will die no more for you. I live that you may not die. Because I live, you shall live also. I reconciled you to my Father by the blood of my cross, and being reconciled you shall live through me. I will pray for you, I will fight for you, I will yet do you good.
　　　　　　　　　　—The Holy War

We sell our earthly happiness
　　For heavenly house and home;
We leave this world because 'tis less,
　　And worse than that to come.

We change our drossy dust for gold;
　　From death to life we fly.
We let go shadows, and take hold
　　Of immortality.

We trade for that which lasting is,
　　And nothing for it give
But that which is already his
　　By whom we breathe and live.

For as the devil sets before
　　Me heaviness and grief,
So God sets Christ and grace much more,
　　Whereby I take relief.

—Prison Meditations

They who in truth come to him, come for what they may receive at his hand. They come for light, they come for life, they come for reconciliation with God. They also come for peace. They come that their souls may be satisfied with spiritual good, and that they may be protected by him against all spiritual and eternal damnation. He alone is able to give them all this, to the fulfilling of their joy.

—Come, and Welcome, to Jesus Christ

Suppose a man is coming to Christ to be saved, and has nothing but sin and an illspent life to bring with him. Let him come, and welcome, to Jesus Christ, "and he will in no wise cast him out" (John 6:37). Is this not a love that passes knowledge? And is not this love the wonderment of angels? And is not this love worthy of all acceptation at the hands and hearts of all coming sinners?   —*Come, and Welcome, to Jesus Christ*

Oh! I saw that my gold was in my trunk at home, in Christ my Lord and Savior. Christ is all—all my righteousness, all my sanctification, and all my redemption.
                    —*Grace Abounding to the Chief of Sinners*

They who are persecutors of the saints of the Lord in this world shall see the Lord's persecuted ones to be those who are so highly esteemed by the Lord as to be in Abraham's bosom. Therefore be not grieved, O you that are tempted, persecuted, afflicted, sighing, praying saints of the Lord. Though your adversaries look upon you now with a disdainful, surly, rugged, proud, and haughty countenance, yet the time shall come when they shall spy you in Abraham's bosom.
                    —*The Groans of a Damned Soul*

If we would live in peace, let us make the best construction of one another's words and actions. Love judges the best, and it thinks no evil. If words and actions may be construed in a good sense, let us never put a bad construction upon them. How much has the peace of Christians been broken by an unloving interpretation of words and actions?
                    —*An Exhortation to Peace and Unity*

Stand for me, my friend, my Mansoul, against the Diabolonians, and I will stand for you before my Father and all his court. Love me against temptation, and I will love you notwithstanding your infirmities.

Nor must you think always to live by sense; you must live upon my word. You must believe, O my Mansoul, that I love you and bear you upon my heart forever.

Remember, O my Mansoul, that you are beloved of me. As I have therefore taught you to watch, to fight, to pray, and to make war against my foes, so now I command you to believe that my love is constant to you. O my Mansoul, how I have set my heart, my love, upon you! Watch. Hold fast till I come.

—The Holy War

Suppose a young man should have his heart much set upon a virgin to have her to wife. If ever he fears he shall not obtain her it is when he begins to love. "Now," thinks he, "somebody will step in betwixt my love and its object. Either they will find fault with my person, my estate, my condition, or something." Now thoughts begin to work: "She does not like me."

And thus it is with the soul at first coming to Jesus Christ. You love him, and your love produces jealousy, and that jealousy often begets fear.

Now you fear the sins of your youth, the sins of your heart. You think something or other will alienate the heart and affections of Jesus Christ from you. You think he sees something in you for the sake of which he will refuse your soul.

But be content; a little more knowledge of him will make you take better heart. You are sick from love, a very sweet disease.

—Come, and Welcome, to Jesus Christ

What fruit have you? Have you fruit becoming the care of God, the protection of God, the wisdom of God, the patience and husbandry of God? It is the fruit of the vineyard that is either the shame or the praise of the husbandman.   —*The Barren Fig Tree*

When I have been in fits of agonies of my spirit, I have been strongly persuaded to seek the Lord no longer. But I have come to understand what great sinners the Lord has had mercy on, and how large his promises still are to sinners, and that it is not the whole but the sick, not the righteous but the sinner, not the full but the empty, unto whom he expends his grace and mercy. This has made me, through the assistance of his Holy Spirit, to cleave to him, to hang upon him, and yet to cry, even though for the present he makes no answer. The Lord helps all his poor, tempted, and afflicted people to continue, though it be long, and helps them pray with the Spirit and with the understanding also.   —*Discourse on Prayer*

God looks for such fruit as is worthy of his name, as is meet for him. We are to show in every place that the presence of God is with us, his fear is in us, and his majesty and authority are upon our actions. Fruits meet for him are: a dependance upon him, trust in his word, and satisfaction in his presence. We are to have such delight in the enjoyment of him that we demonstrate his fear is in our hearts and that our souls are wrapped up in his things.   —*The Barren Fig Tree*

A man must be good or else he can bring forth no good fruit. He must have righteousness imputed so that he may stand good in God's sight from the curse of his law. He must have a principle of righteousness in his soul or else how will he bring forth good fruit? A Christian's fruits are called fruits of the Spirit, the fruits of righteousness which are by Jesus Christ. To be the fruits of the Spirit, the Spirit must be there. To be the fruits of righteousness, righteousness must first be there. *—The Barren Fig Tree*

Faithful: How does the saving grace of God discover itself when it is in the heart of man?

Talkative: I perceive that our talk must be about the *power* of things. First, where the grace of God is in the heart it causes there a great outcry against sin. Secondly—

Faithful: Nay, hold; let us consider of one at once. I think you should rather say it shows itself by inclining the soul to abhor its sin.

Talkative: Why, what difference is there between crying out against and abhorring of sin?

Faithful: Oh, a great deal! A man may cry out against sin, but he cannot abhor it except by virtue of a godly antipathy against it. I have heard many cry out against sin in the pulpit who yet can abide it well enough in the heart, house, and conversation. Joseph's mistress cried with a loud voice as if she had been very holy, but she would willingly, notwithstanding that, have committed uncleanness with him (Gen. 39:11-15). *—The Pilgrim's Progress*

If you would so run as to obtain the kingdom of heaven, then be sure that you get into the way that leads there. For it is a vain thing to think that you shall have the prize, though you run ever so fast, unless you are in the way that leads to it. Set the case that there should be a man in London who was to run to York for a wager. Now, though he run ever so swiftly, yet if he run full south he might run himself quickly out of breath and be never the nearer the prize, but rather the farther off. Just so it is here. It is not simply the runner, nor yet the hasty runner, that wins the crown unless he be in the way that leads thereto. I have observed during the little time which I have been a believer that there is a great running to and fro, some this way and some that way. Yet it is to be feared that most of them are out of the way, and though they run as swift as the eagle can fly, they are benefited nothing at all.   —*The Heavenly Footman*

Manasseh was a bad man and Magdalen a bad woman, to say nothing of the thief upon the cross or of the murderers of Christ. Yet they obtained mercy; Christ willingly received them.

And do you think that those, once so bad, now that they are in heaven repent that they are there because they left their sins for Christ when they were in the world? Christ at heaven's gates says to you, "Come thither." And the devil, at the gates of hell, calls you to come to him. Sinner, where will you go? Don't go into the fire; there you will be burned. Do not let Jesus lose his longing, since it is for your salvation, but come to him and live.   —*The Jerusalem Sinner Saved*

Never think that to live always in Christ for justification is a low and beggarly thing, and, as it were, a staying at the foundation. For let me tell you, depart from a sense of the meritorious means of your justification with God and you will quickly grow light and frothy and vain. Besides, you will always be subject to errors and delusions.

Further, no man that builds forsakes the good foundation. That is the ground of his encouragement to work. For upon that is laid the stress of all, and without it nothing that is framed can be supported, but must inevitably fall to the ground. Again, why not live upon Christ always, especially since he stands as the mediator between God and the soul, defending you with the merit of his blood and covering you with his infinite righteousness from the wrath of God and curse of the law.

Can there be any greater comfort ministered to you than to know that you stand just before God—just, and justified from all things that would otherwise swallow you up? Is peace with God and assurance of heaven of so little respect to you that you slight the very foundation thereof, even faith in the blood and righteousness of Christ? And are notions and whimsies of such credit with you that you must leave the foundation to follow them? But again, what mystery is desirable to be known that is not to be found in Jesus Christ, as priest, prophet, or king of saints? "In whom are hid all the treasures of wisdom and knowledge" (Col. 2:3).

—*Justification by an Imputed Righteousness*

A life of holiness and godliness in this world does so inseparably follow a principle of faith that it is both monstrous and ridiculous to suppose the contrary.

—*Christian Behavior*

Your neighbors are diligent for things that will perish. Will you be slothful for things that will endure forever?

—*An Epistle*

In times of affliction we commonly meet with the sweetest experience of the love of God.

—*Bunyan's Dying Sayings (of Affliction)*

I have often thought that the best of Christians are found in the worst of times. And I have thought that one reason why we are no better is because God purges us no more. Noah and Lot—who were as holy as they in the time of their afflictions? And yet who were as idle as they in the time of their prosperity?

—*Bunyan's Dying Sayings (of Suffering)*

I remember that one day as I was traveling into the country and musing on the wickedness and blasphemy of my heart, and considering the enmity that was in me toward God, this Scripture came into my mind: "And, having made peace through the blood of his cross, by him to reconcile all things unto himself" (Col. 1:20). By those words I was made to see again and again that day that God and my soul were friends by his blood. Yea, I saw that the justice of God and my sinful soul could embrace and kiss each other through his blood. This was a good day to me; I hope I shall never forget it.

—Grace Abounding to the Chief of Sinners

Chapter Eleven

WHO WEARS THE CROWN?

"Christ is the desire of nations, the joy of angels, the delight of the Father."

world of wonders! (I can say no less.)
That I should be preserved in that distress
That I have met with here! Oh blessed be
That hand which from it has delivered me!
Dangers in darkness, devils, hell, and sin
Did compass me while I this vale was in.
Yea, snares and pits and traps and nets did lie
My path about, that worthless, silly I
Might have been caught, entangled, and cast down;
But since I live, let Jesus wear the crown.

                              —*The Pilgrim's Progress*

The man who comes to Christ is one who has had deep considerations of his own sins, slighting thoughts of his own righteousness, and high thoughts of the blood and righteousness of Jesus Christ. Yea, he sees more virtue in the blood of Christ to save him than there is in all his sins to damn him. He therefore sets Christ before his eyes. There is nothing in heaven or earth, he knows, that can save his soul and secure him from the wrath of God, but Christ.

                              —*Come, and Welcome, to Jesus Christ*

Shall I lose a long heaven for a short pleasure? Shall I buy the pleasures of this world at so dear a rate as to lose my soul for their obtaining? Shall I content myself with a heaven that will last no longer than my lifetime? What advantage will these be to me when the Lord shall separate soul and body asunder and send one to the grave and the other to hell, and at the judgment day the final sentence of eternal ruin must be passed upon me? —*The Groans of a Damned Soul*

There is flesh as well as spirit in the best of saints. And as the spirit of grace will be always putting forth something that is good, so the flesh will be putting forth that which is evil. —*Christian Behavior*

Many have spoken of it, but none can tell what the valley of the Shadow of Death should mean until they come in themselves.
—*The Pilgrim's Progress, Part II*

He who lives in sin and looks for happiness hereafter is like him that sows cockle and thinks to fill his barn with wheat and barley.
—*The Pilgrim's Progress, Part II*

'Tis easier watching a night or two than to sit up a whole year together. So 'tis easier for one to begin to profess well than to hold out as he should to the end. —*The Pilgrim's Progress, Part II*

He that has the hearts of men in his hand can change them from worse to better. May God give long life to them that are good, and especially to those of them who are capable of doing him service in the world. The ornament and beauty of this lower world, next to God and his wonders, are the men who spangle and shine in godliness.

—The Life and Death of Mr. Badman

Consider that the getting of wealth dishonestly (as he does who gets it without good conscience and charity to his neighbor) is a great offense against God. But a little honesty gotten, though it may yield you but a dinner of herbs at a time, will yield more peace than a stalled ox ill gotten. Better is a little with righteousness than great revenues without right. Be confident that God's eyes are upon all your ways.

—The Life and Death of Mr. Badman

The Lord Mayor of the town of Mansoul stood at the gate of the King's Court desiring to be admitted into the presence of the Prince, the King's Son. But the Prince would not come down nor declare that the gate should be opened to him, but sent him an answer to this effect: "They have turned their backs upon me, and not their faces; but now in the time of their trouble they say unto me, 'Arise, and save us.' But can they not now go to Mr. Carnal-security, to whom they went when they turned from me, and make him their leader, their lord, and their protector? Why now in their trouble do they visit me since in their prosperity they went astray?"

—The Holy War

124

Righteousness still resides in and with the person of Christ, for we are justified in him. The righteousness is still in him, not in us, even when we are made partakers of its benefit, as the wing and feathers still abide in the hen when the chickens are covered, kept, and warmed thereby.

For as my doings, though my children are fed and clothed thereby, are still my doings, not theirs, so the righteousness wherewith we stand just before God still resides in Christ, not in us. Our sins, when laid upon Christ, were yet personally ours, not his; so his righteousness, when put upon us, is yet personally his, not ours. What is it then? Why, "He hath made him to be sin for us, who knew no sin; that we might be made the righteousness of God in him" (2 Cor. 5:21).

—Justification by an Imputed Righteousness

It was not my good frame of heart that made my righteousness better nor yet my bad frame that made my righteousness worse, for my righteousness was Jesus Christ himself: the same yesterday, today, and for ever (Heb. 13:8).

—Grace Abounding to the Chief of Sinners

In my preaching I have really been in pain and have travailed to bring forth children to God. Neither could I be satisfied unless some fruits did appear in my work. If I were fruitless, it mattered not who commended me; but if I were fruitful, I cared not who did condemn.

—Grace Abounding to the Chief of Sinners

I have observed that where I have had a work to do for God I have had first the moving of God upon my spirit to desire I might preach there. I have also observed that such and such souls in particular have been strongly set upon my heart and I stirred up to wish for their salvation, and that these very souls have been given as the fruits of my ministry. I have observed that a word cast in by the by has done more execution in a sermon than all that was spoken besides. Sometimes, also, when I have thought I did no good then I did the most of all, and at other times when I thought I should catch them, I have fished for nothing.

—Grace Abounding to the Chief of Sinners

God is never weary of being delighted with Jesus Christ; his blood is always precious with God.

—Justification by an Imputed Righteousness

Christ is the desire of nations, the joy of angels, the delight of the Father. With what solace then the soul is filled that has the possession of him to all eternity!

—Bunyan's Dying Sayings

Thus far did I come laden with my sin,
Nor could aught ease the grief that I was in
Till I came hither; what a place is this!
Must here be the beginning of my bliss?
Must here the burden fall from off my back?
Must here the strings that bind it to me crack?
Blessed cross, blessed sepulchre; blessed rather be
The Man that there was put to shame for me!
                                    —*The Pilgrim's Progress*

Chapter Twelve

A FINE-SPUN THREAD

"Therefore, to live by faith is so much the harder work, yet it must be done; otherwise your other duties profit you nothing."

Make conscience of the duty of believing, and be as afraid of falling short here as in any other command of God. This is the will of God, that you believe. Believe, therefore, to the saving of the soul. Unbelief is a fine-spun thread, not so easily discerned as grosser sins, and therefore it is truly the sin that does so easily beset us. The light of nature will show those sins that are against the law of nature, but the law of faith is a command beyond what flesh or nature teaches.

Therefore, to live by faith is so much the harder work, yet it must be done; otherwise your other duties profit you nothing. Your other duties: prayer, alms, thanksgiving, self-denial, or any other, will be hard for you to prove. Remember that faith pleases God and that without faith it is impossible to please him.

—Justification by an Imputed Righteousness

To be truly sensible about sin is to sorrow for displeasing God. It is to be afflicted that he is displeased by us more than that he is displeased with us.

—Bunyan's Dying Sayings
(of Repentance and Coming to Christ)

The mole's a creature very smooth and slick.
She digs in the dirt, but 'twill not on her stick.
So's he who counts this world his greatest gains,
Yet nothing gets but labor for his pains.
Earth's the mole's element; she can't abide
To be above ground—dirt heaps are her pride.
And he is like her who the worldling plays;
He imitates her in her works and ways.

Poor willy mole, that you should love to be
Where you nor sun nor moon nor stars can see.
But oh, how silly's he who does not care—
So he gets earth—to have of heaven a share!

—*Of the Mole in the Ground*

I am not come to put Mansoul upon works to live thereby, but I am come that by me and by what I have and shall do for Mansoul they may be reconciled to my Father, though by their sin they have provoked him to anger and by the law they cannot obtain mercy.

—*The Holy War*

Look, look, brave Sol doth peep up from beneath,
Shows us his golden face, doth on us breathe.
Yea, he doth compass us around with glories
While he ascends up to his highest stories
Where he his banner over us displays
And gives us light to see our works and ways.

Nor are we now, as at the peep of light
To question is it day or is it night?
The night is gone, the shadow's fled away,
And now we are most certain that 'tis day.

And thus it is when Jesus shows his face,
And doth assure us of his love and grace.

—*On the Rising of the Sun*

The gospel here has had a summer's day,
But in its sunshine we, like fools, did play,
Or else fall out and with each other wrangle,
And did, instead of work, not much but jangle.

And if our sun seems angry, hides his face,
Shall it go down—shall night possess this place?
Let not the voice of night-birds us afflict,
And of our misspent summer us convict.
—Of the Going Down of the Sun

Did we heartily renounce the pleasures of this world, we should be very little troubled for our afflictions. That which renders an afflicted state so insupportable to many is because they are too much addicted to the pleasures of this life and so cannot endure that which makes a separation between them.
—Bunyan's Dying Sayings (of Affliction)

Despair is an unprofitable thing; it will make a man weary of waiting upon God. It will make a man forsake God, and seek his heaven in the good things of this world. It will make a man his own tormentor, and flounce and fling like a wild beast in a net.
Despair! It drives a man to the study of his own ruin, and brings him at last to his own executioner.
—The Jerusalem Sinner Saved

A word of advice to all God's people. Believe that as surely as you are in the way of God you must meet temptations. The first day that you enter Christ's congregation, look for them. When they come, beg God to carry you through them.

Grace be with you. *—Discourse on Prayer*

Some men, when they come to the cross, can go no farther, but back again to their sins they go. Others stumble and break their necks. Others, when they see that the cross is approaching, turn aside to the left hand or to the right hand, and so think to get to heaven another way. But they will be deceived.

There are but few when they come to the cross who cry, "Welcome, cross," as some of the martyrs did at the stake where they were burned. Therefore if you meet with the cross in your journey, be not daunted and say, "Alas, what shall I do now!" But rather take courage, knowing that the cross is the way to the kingdom.

Can a man believe in Christ and not be hated by the devil? Can he make a profession of this Christ, sweetly and convincingly, and the children of Satan hold their tongues? Can darkness agree with light? Can the devil endure that Christ Jesus be honored both by faith and a heavenly conversation? Christ said, "In the world ye shall have tribulation" (John 16:33).

—The Heavenly Footman

Temptations, when we meet them at first, are as the lion that roared at Samson. But if we overcome them, then the next time we see them we shall find a nest of honey within them.

—Grace Abounding to the Chief of Sinners

Love your Savior! Yea, show to one another that you love him, not only by a seeming love of affection but with the love of duty. Practical love is best. Many love Christ with nothing but the lick of the tongue. Alas! Christ Jesus the Lord must not be put off this way. "He that hath my commandments, and keepeth them," says he, "he it is that loveth me" (John 14:21).

—The Jerusalem Sinner Saved

My Mansoul, I have oftentimes delivered you from the designs, plots, attempts, and conspiracies of Diabolus. For all this I ask nothing but that you render not to me evil for my good, and that you bear in mind my love and the continuation of my kindness. Walk according to the benefits bestowed on you.

—The Holy War

I found that I loved Christ dearly. Oh, my soul cleaved to him, my affections cleaved to him. I felt my love to him as hot as fire. But I quickly found that my great love was but little, and that I who had, as I thought, such burning love for Jesus Christ could let him go again for a very trifle.

—Grace Abounding to the Chief of Sinners

Chapter Thirteen

HERE COME THE ANGELS, HERE COME THE SAINTS

"Not by works of righteousness which we have done, but according to his mercy he saved us."

ere come the angels, here come the saints,
Here comes the spirit of God
To comfort us in our restraints
Under the wicked's rod.   *—Prison Meditations*

When God intends to stock a place with saints, and to make that place flourish with the riches of his grace, he usually begins with the conversion of some of the most notorious thereabouts, and makes them an example to allure others.   *—The Jerusalem Sinner Saved*

The bands of the gospel are goodness, with which men love to be bound, and by such as they pray they may hold fast. He binds his foal to the vine, his saint unto his Savior.   *—Solomon's Temple Revisited*

138

Christ can bear with your weakness, he can pity your ignorance, he can be touched with the feeling of your infirmities, he can affectionately forgive your trans-gressions, he can heal your backsliding and love you freely. His compassions fail not: "A bruised reed shall he not break, and the smoking flax shall he not quench" (Isa. 42:3). He can pity them which no eye pities, and be afflicted in all your afflictions.

—Come, and Welcome, to Jesus Christ

I concluded that a little grace, a little love, a little of the true fear of God, is better than all the gifts. I am fully convinced that it is possible for souls that can scarce give a man an answer to have a thousand times more grace, and to be more in the love and favor of the Lord, than some who by the virtue of the gift of knowledge can deliver themselves like angels.

—Grace Abounding to the Chief of Sinners

The materials with which the temple was built were in their own nature common to that which was left behind, things that were not fit, without art, to be laid in so holy a house. This shows that those of whom Christ Jesus designs to build his church are by nature no better than others. But as the trees and stones of which the temple was built were first hewed and squared before they were fit to be laid in that house, so sinners, of which the church is to be built, must first be fitted by the Word and doctrine, and then fitly laid in their place in the church.

—Solomon's Temple Spiritualized

All imperfection arises from the badness of the heart, but there will be no bad hearts in glory. No shortness of knowledge, no cross dispositions, no lusts or corruptions will be there; no, not throughout the whole heavens. Here these are seen in the best of saints because here our light is mixed with darkness, but in heaven there will be no night.

—*Solomon's Temple Spiritualized*

The saints of old—willing and resolved for heaven—what could stop them? Could fire and faggot, sword or halter, filthy dungeons, whips, bears, bulls, lions, cruel rackings, stoning, starving, nakedness? In all these things they were more than conquerors through him that loved them. —*The Heavenly Footman*

The children of the devil, because they are not willing, have many shifts and starting holes: "I have married a wife, I have a farm, I shall offend my landlord, I shall offend my master, I shall lose my trading, I shall lose my pride, my pleasures, I shall be mocked and scoffed; therefore I dare not come." Says another, "I will wait till I am older, till my children are out, till I have done this and that and the other business." But, alas, the thing is they are not willing. For were they but soundly willing, these excuses, and a thousand such as these, would hold them no longer than the cords held Samson when he broke them like burnt flax.

—*The Heavenly Footman*

It was not the worthiness of Abraham, or Moses, or David, or Peter, or Paul, but the mercy of God, that made them inheritors of heaven. If God thinks you worthy, judge not yourself unworthy; take it, and be thankful.

—Come, and Welcome, to Jesus Christ

No man will lay trees as they come from the wood for beams and rafters in his house, nor stones as digged in the walls. No, the trees must be hewed and squared, and the stones sawn and made fit, and so be laid in the house. Yea, they must be so sawn and so squared that in coupling they may be joined exactly, else the building will not be good nor the workman have credit of his doings. Hence our gospel church is fitly formed, and there is a fit supply of every joint for the securing of the whole.

As they therefore build like children who build with wood as it comes from the wood or forest, and with stones as they come from the pit, even so do they who pretend to build God a house of unconverted sinners, unhewed, unsquared, unpolished. Let ministers therefore look to this and take heed, lest instead of making their notions stoop to the word they make the Scriptures stoop to their notions.

—Solomon's Temple Spiritualized

The believer is the man by whom God shows to the world the power of his grace. Unbelievers read indeed the power of grace, of the faith, hope, love, joy, peace, and sanctification of the heart of the Christian, but they feel nothing of that sin-killing operation that is in these things. These are to them as a story of Rome or Spain. Therefore, to show them in others what they find not in themselves, God works faith, hope, love, etc., in a generation that shall serve him, and by them they shall see what they cannot find in themselves. By this means they shall be convinced that though sin and the pleasures of this life be sweet to them, yet there is a people otherwise minded, even such a people that do indeed see the glory of that which others read of, and from that light take pleasure in those things unto which they are most averse. To this, I say, are Christians called. Herein is God glorified; hereby are sinners convinced, and by this is the world condemned.

—Christian Behavior

There is nothing more seemly in this world than to see a Christian walk as becomes the gospel, nor anything more unbecoming a reasonable creature than to hear a man say, "I believe in Christ," and yet see in his life debauchery and profaneness.

—The Jerusalem Sinner Saved

Living by faith begets in the heart a son-like boldness and confidence to God in all our gospel duties, under all our weaknesses and under all our temptations. It is a blessed thing to be privileged with holy boldness and confidence toward God, to know that he is on our side, that he takes part with us and that he will plead our cause with them that rise up against us.

But this boldness is what faith helps us to do. This is what made Paul always triumph and rejoice in God. He lived the life of faith, for faith sets a man in the favor of God by Christ. Faith makes a man see that what befalls him in this life shall, through the wisdom and mercy of God, not only provide for his forwarding to heaven but augment his glory when he comes there. This man now stands on high. He is rid of slavish fears and carking cares, and in all his straits he has God to go to.   —*Justification by an Imputed Righteousness*

Men at first conversion are like a cake well baked and newly taken from the oven; they are warm and cast forth a very fragrant scent.

—*Solomon's Temple Spiritualized*

The Word of God took hold of my heart: "Being justified freely by his grace through the redemption that is in Christ Jesus" (Rom. 3:24). What an effect it made upon me!

I was as one awaked out of some troublesome sleep and dream. It was as if I had heard it said to me: "Sinner, you think that because of your sins and infirmities I cannot save your soul. But behold, my Son is by me, and I look upon him and not on you. I shall deal with you according as I am pleased with him." At this I was greatly enlightened in my mind and made to understand that, if God could justify a sinner at any time, it was by his looking upon Christ and imputing of his benefits to me that the work was forthwith done.

And, as I was musing, that Scripture also came with great power upon my spirit: "Not by works of righteousness which we have done, but according to his mercy he saved us" (Titus 3:5). Now was I lifted high; I saw myself within the arms of grace and mercy.

—*Grace Abounding to the Chief of Sinners*

Chapter Fourteen

IT IS BETTER GOING TO HEAVEN

"Friend, it is a sad thing to sit down before we are in heaven and to grow weary before we come to the place of rest."

onsider yourself and say, it is better going to heaven than hell; it is better to be saved than damned. It is better to be with saints than with damned souls; to go to God is better than to go to the devil.

Therefore, "Seek ye the Lord while he may be found; call ye upon him while he is near" (Isa. 55:6).

Oh, if they who are in hell might now again have one such invitation as this, how they would leap for joy! I have thought, sometimes, should God send but one of his ministers to the damned in hell, and give him commission to preach the free love of God in Christ, how welcome would he make this news. They would close in with it on any terms!

—*The Groans of a Damned Soul*

Oh, that they who have heard me speak could see as I do what sin, death, hell, and the curse of God is. And what the grace, love, and mercy of God is through Christ toward men estranged from him. Indeed, I did often say in my heart before the Lord that if to be hanged up before their eyes would be a means to awaken them, I gladly should be contented.

—*Grace Abounding to the Chief of Sinners*

Heaven is but a fable to some, and things here are counted the only things substantial. Earthly things, when they are with power upon men's minds, carry their hearts away from God.

—The Pilgrim's Progress, Part II

Talkative thinks that *hearing* and *saying* will make a good Christian, and thus he deceives his own soul. Hearing is but as the sowing of the seed; talking is not sufficient to prove that fruit is indeed the heart and life. Let us assure ourselves that at the day of doom men shall be judged according to their fruits; it will not be said then, "Did you believe?" but "Were you *doers*, or *talkers* only?" Accordingly shall they be judged. The end of the world is compared to our harvest, and you know men at harvest regard nothing but fruit. I speak this to show you how insignificant the profession of Talkative will be at that day.

—The Pilgrim's Progress

Without repentance a man is sure to die in his sin. Sin will lie down in the dust with him, rise at the judgment with him, hang about his neck like cords and chains when he stands at the bar of God's tribunal, and go with him too when he goes away from the judgment seat with a "Depart from me, ye cursed, into everlasting fire prepared for the devil and his angels." There shall his sins fret and gnaw his conscience because they will be to him a never-dying worm.

—The Life and Death of Mr. Badman

The King called to Emmanuel, his Son, who said, "Here am I, my Father."

Then said the King, "Thou knowest, as I do myself, the condition of the town of Mansoul, and what we have purposed and what you have done to redeem it. Come now, my Son, and prepare yourself for the war, for you shall go to my camp at Mansoul. You shall prosper there and prevail, and shall conquer the town of Mansoul."

Then said the King's Son, "Thy law is within my heart. I delight to do thy will. This is the day that I have longed for and the work that I have waited for all this while. Grant me, therefore, what force thou shalt in thy wisdom think meet, and I will go and will deliver from Diabolus and from his power thy perishing town of Mansoul. My heart has been often pained within me for the miserable town of Mansoul, but now it is rejoiced, now it is glad."

And with that he leaped over the mountains for joy, saying, "I have not, in my heart, thought anything too dear for Mansoul. The day of vengeance is in my heart for thee, my Mansoul, and glad am I that thou my Father hast made me the captain of their salvation."

—*The Holy War*

There is no man, I think, who is aware of the worth of one soul but must, when he hears of the death of unconverted men, be stricken with sorrow and grief.

—*The Life and Death of Mr. Badman*

Seriously, will it not grieve you, trouble, perplex, and torment you, when you see that you lost heaven for a little pleasure and profit in your lifetime? Certainly it will grieve you and perplex you exceedingly to see what a blessed heaven you left for a dunghill world. Oh, if you would believe this, and say within yourself: "What, shall I be contented with my portion in this world? What, shall I lose heaven for this world?" I say, consider it while you have daylight and gospel light.   —*The Groans of a Damned Soul*

The Lord should send two or three of his servants, the ministers of the gospel, to hell among the damned with this commission: "Go to hell and preach my grace to those who are there. Let your sermon be an hour long, and hold forth the merits of my Son's birth, righteousness, death, resurrection, ascension, and intercession, with all my love in him. Proffer it to them. Tell them that now once do I proffer the means of reconciliation to them." They who are now roaring, being past hope, would leap at the least proffer of mercy.

Mercy would be welcome when souls are under judgment. Now this soul is in the fire; now he is under the wrath of God; now he is in hell, there to be tormented; now he is with the devils and damned spirits; now he feels the vengeance of God. Now, oh now, you may see that mercy is prized by them that are in hell; they would be glad if they could have it.

—*The Groans of a Damned Soul*

It is he that holds out to the end who will be saved. It is he who overcomes who shall inherit all things; it is not every one who begins. Agrippa gave a fair step; he stepped almost into the bosom of Christ in less than half an hour. "Almost (he said to Paul) thou persuadest me to be a Christian" (Acts 26:28).

Ah, but it was but almost. He stepped fair indeed, but yet he stopped short; he was hot while he was at it, but he was quickly out of wind—almost into the kingdom, almost out of the hands of the devil, almost out from under the curse of God.

Almost, and that was all. Almost, but not altogether. Friend, it is a sad thing to sit down before we are in heaven and to grow weary before we come to the place of rest.   —*The Heavenly Footman*

This coming to Christ is called a running to him, a flying to him. Men will consider if there is any other way of escape before they fly. Therefore flying is the last thing. When all refuge fails, and a man is made to see that there is nothing left to him but sin, death, and damnation unless he flies to Christ for life, then he flies, but not till then.

   —*Come, and Welcome, to Jesus Christ*

152

Poor sinner, awake! Eternity is coming, and his Son; they are both coming to judge the world. Awake! Are you yet asleep, poor sinner? Let me set the trumpet to your ear once again. The heavens will shortly be a burning flame; the earth, and the works thereof, shall be burned up. Then wicked men shall go into perdition. Do you hear this, sinner? The sweet morsels of sin will then be gone, and only their bitter burning fruits left.

What do you say now, sinner? Can you drink hell fire? Will the wrath of God be a pleasant dish to your taste? This will be your every day's meat and drink in hell, sinner.

I will yet propound to you God's ponderous question, and then for this time leave you: "Can thine heart endure, or can thine hands be strong, in the days that I shall deal with thee?" (Ezek. 22:16) says the Lord. What do you say? Will you answer this question now?

—*The Strait Gate*

Index

l

1